TEACHER'S BOOK

Highly Recommended

English for the hotel and catering industry

NEW EDITION

Trish Stott & Rod Revell

OXFORD
UNIVERSITY PRESS

Introduction

Aims of the course

Highly Recommended is designed to improve the job-related English of people who are training for, or who have already started, careers in the hotel and catering industry. The functional aspects of the course describe the work routines of receptionists, porters, room attendants, waiters, waitresses, and bar and kitchen staff. The course covers a variety of situations where employees have to use English with both customers and other members of staff.

The course is intended for students starting at the post-elementary level of language but the material can be easily adapted for classes of mixed-ability. See below for suggestions on how to do this.

Structure of the course

The course consists of a Student's Book, Teacher's Book, Workbook, and listening material. The Student's Book consists of twenty-eight units which take the student through a number of hotel and restaurant situations and functions, beginning with phone enquiries and reservations through to payments and queries. The final two units deal with aspects of job applications and interviews. In addition to the functional focus, each unit identifies a vocabulary area and particular language points for study. Functions and structures are summarized in the Contents chart in the Student's Book, also reproduced here on pages 4–5.

The functional language of the unit is summarized under the unit title. Some students may already be familiar with these phrases. The teacher can return to them at the end of the unit to check that objectives have been achieved. They are also useful for a quick recycling of language from previously completed units. Revision suggestions are given at the beginning of each unit of the Teacher's Book. At least 5–10 minutes' revision is recommended for each 90-minute lesson.

Giving your students adequate revision time is also particularly important if the level of your class is mixed-ability. The ratio of strong to weak students will determine exactly where you choose to pitch the material. Having a mixed-ability class means there will also be problems such as classroom management and lack of motivation. Here are some suggestions for resolving these problems with weaker students:

- encourage weaker and stronger students to work together
- allow weaker students more 'rehearsal time' before speaking activities
- allow weaker students to use their first language more often
- build in more writing stages before speaking activities
- allocate 'low pressure' roles to weaker students. For example, *secretary* (to collect ideas) or *scribe* (to write results of a discussion on the board).

Here are some suggestions for stronger students:

- give stronger students a shorter time limit to complete exercises and activities
- insist on effective pronunciation and intonation from stronger students during speaking activities
- challenge stronger students with extra vocabulary or different parts of speech
- have extra exercises ready for fast finishers
- give stronger students extended dictionary skills work
- allocate 'high pressure' roles to stronger students. For example, *organizer* (in an activity) or *chairperson* (in a discussion).

Each unit is divided into the following sections:

Starter

This is intended as a warm-up to each unit. The activity usually relates to the photograph or picture at the beginning of each unit and gives weaker students a chance to participate by contributing information in their first language, which can then be taught in English if appropriate. This section is an opportunity for the teacher to get students' attention and enthusiasm by personalizing the material, and encouraging them to contribute from their own knowledge and experience.

Listening

This is a dialogue or series of dialogues on the theme indicated by the title of the unit. Some of the Listening sections contain specialist vocabulary and so are quite demanding. It is important, therefore, to prepare students well before they listen. Pre-teach unfamiliar vocabulary and practise the pronunciation of items that students will have to recognize in order to complete the tasks. They will often need to listen to the recording more than once in order to complete a task. Answers to the tasks are given in the teaching notes at the relevant point. The final activity of each of these Listening sections is for students to practise the dialogues in pairs, using the **Listening scripts** at the back of their books.

Language study

Expressions to learn begins this section, and is a list of useful expressions from the first Listening. As a result, you may wish to ask students to cover this box while they are doing the preceding listening exercises. Most unfamiliar vocabulary will be found in the **Wordlist** at the back of the Student's Book in French, German, Italian, Spanish, and Japanese. The expressions are also labelled to indicate whether they are usually spoken by customers or staff, or in Units 27 and 28, the applicant or interviewer.

New words to use is an alphabetical list of the new words in the unit. These words are all translated in the **Wordlist**. You will also want to draw students' attention to the **Useful vocabulary** on page 110, which features food groups, ordinal numbers, and a telephone alphabet.

The section concludes with **Structures to practise**, which introduces and practises points of grammar or a significant language area already met in the Listening section. There are useful supplementary notes and exercises in the **Language review** section at the back of the Student's Book. These can be done as written work in class, or given as homework but answers should be read aloud by students around the class. The teacher should check both pronunciation and intonation. In addition, there is a list of **Irregular verbs** on page 111 of the Student's Book.

The second Listening

This expands the theme of the unit and provides further listening practice. For more guidance, see the notes to Listening above.

Activity

This consists of improvisations, role-plays, and information gap activities based on the vocabulary and structures contained in the unit. In the case of improvisations and role-plays, Student A's information is usually in the unit; Student B's information is usually at the back of the Student's Book. The activities are designed to provide fluency practice. Therefore, students should not write the dialogues beforehand. Most activities can be set up in a similar way:

Ask students to form pairs or groups and tell them to look at the relevant information. Where appropriate, make sure they do not look at each other's information. Model important and useful phrases and ask students to repeat them chorally and individually. Check pronunciation and intonation. While students are doing the Activity, go around the class, checking and giving help where necessary. Make a note of any mistakes, particularly in language already learnt, and write these on the board afterwards for students to correct. Finally, you could ask pairs or groups of students to perform in front of the class.

More words to use

These lists of words complete or extend word groups already learnt in the unit. They stimulate and encourage students to expand their vocabulary in related topic areas. Except for word groups like numbers, days of the week, and months, these words also appear in the **Wordlist**.

The **Help yourself** section (pages 92–6) should be used as revision and personalization at the end of the course. There is no Answer key for this section, but students should be encouraged to revise useful language for their own particular situations.

Unit contents chart

UNIT	COMMUNICATIVE AREA	SITUATIONS/FUNCTIONS	STRUCTURES
1	Taking phone calls	Incoming calls: *James speaking. How can I help?* Making simple requests: *Can/Could I reserve a parking space? I'd like to speak to Mrs Bader.*	Requests with *Can/Could*, *I'd like to*
2	Giving information	Hotel and restaurant location and facilities: *There are more than 900 bedrooms on eight floors.* Identifying yourself: *My name's Caroline.*	Present Simple of *be*: *Is there?/Are there?*, *There is/There are*, *There isn't/There aren't*
3	Taking room reservations	Requesting information: *Do you have a double room? Does the hotel have a restaurant?*	*Do, Does* Prepositions of time: *on, at, in, from ... to*
4	Taking restaurant bookings	Opening and closing times: *When do you close? What time do you serve dinner?*	Dates Adverbs of frequency: *always, often, sometimes, rarely, never*
5	Giving polite explanations	Turning down requests: *I'm sorry,/afraid we're fully booked that weekend.*	Present Simple (short forms): *be, do, can*
6	Receiving guests	Guests arriving at hotel reception or restaurant: *Could you fill in this registration card? Here's your key card.*	Possessive adjectives: *my, your, his, her, our, your, their*
7	Serving in the bar	In the bar: *What can I get you?* Requests and offers: *Would you like ice and lemon?*	Requests and offers with *Can, Could, Shall, Would you like?*
8	Instructions	Mixing a cocktail: *How do you make a Margarita?* Giving instructions in sequence: *First, take a cocktail shaker and fill it with crushed ice. Next, pour in one measure of tequila.*	Instructions: *take, fill, pour* Sequence markers: *first, next, then, finally*
9	Taking a food order	Restaurant staff taking orders for aperitifs, starters, and main courses: *Are you ready to order? Would you like to order some wine?*	*a/an, the* *a/an, some*
10	Desserts and cheese	Restaurant staff explaining cheese and dessert menus: *I recommend the French apple tart. The lemon tart is very good, too. What kind of cheese is Stilton?*	*some, any*
11	Talking about wine	Restaurant wine waiter taking orders: *The Sauvignon Blanc is drier than the Riesling.*	Comparisons: *-er than, more ... than, not as ... as*
12	Dealing with requests	Hotel reception and restaurant staff replying to requests: *I'll get you some more. I'll bring you another.*	Offering help: *I'll get you some/one/another/some more.*
13	Describing dishes	Waiter explaining menu: *It contains/consists of/is made of pasta.*	Present Simple Passive
14	Dealing with complaints	Guests complaining in a hotel and restaurant: *We ordered our drinks twenty minutes ago.*	Past Simple
15	Jobs and workplaces	Hotel reception and kitchen staff explaining responsibilities: *This is Louise. She's responsible for six staff.*	*this/that, these/those, here/there* *responsible to, responsible for*

UNIT	COMMUNICATIVE AREA	SITUATIONS/FUNCTIONS	STRUCTURES
16	Explaining and instructing	Hotel kitchen staff instructing trainee: *First, you must wash your hands. You have to break it into florets. It mustn't cook for long.*	*must, have to, don't have to, musn't*
17	Taking telephone requests	Hotel facilities and services: *How many glasses do you need? My suit needs dry cleaning. We need to leave in half an hour.*	*need* + noun *need* + *-ing* *need* + full infinitive
18	Taking difficult phone calls	Hotel reception taking difficult phone reservations: *I'm sorry, I didn't catch the date. Can you speak up?*	Past Simple: questions and short answers, and negative statements
19	Health and safety at work	Hotel assistant manager reading safety regulations: *Please read the list carefully.*	Adjectives and adverbs
20	Giving directions indoors	Hotel staff directing guests: *It's on the ground floor. Take the lift to the first floor.*	Prepositions of location and direction (1)
21	Giving directions outside	Hotel staff directing guests: *It's quite near here. Turn right outside the hotel. Take the tube from here.*	Prepositions of location and direction (2)
22	Facilities for the business traveller	Hotel reception explaining conference facilities to a guest: *Can you tell me about your in-room facilities?*	Linking and contrasting: *so, both ... and, but*
23	Offering help and advice	Hotel staff dealing with an accident: *One of the guests has just fallen over. We should call an ambulance.*	Present Perfect with *yet, just* *should* for advice
24	Dealing with problems	Hotel guests complaining to reception: *My room hasn't been serviced. It should have been done this morning.*	*should* + Present Perfect Passive
25	Paying bills	Hotel and restaurant payments: *How are you paying? Would you like a VAT receipt?*	Present Continuous Object pronouns: *me, you, him, her, it, you, us, them*
26	Payment queries	Hotel and restaurant guests querying bills: *I think there's a mistake. How much is the minibar bill?*	*much, many, a lot of*
27	Applying for a job	Writing a CV	Formal language for business letters and applications: *Dear Sir/Madam, Yours faithfully/sincerely*
28	The interview	A job interview: *I think I have the right skills and experience for the job. I'm going to make a shortlist. I'm seeing three more candidates tomorrow.*	Talking about the future: *will, going to, -ing*

Activity material	60	Wordlist	97	
Listening scripts	66	Useful vocabulary	110	
Language review	76	Irregular verbs	111	
Help yourself	92			

1 Taking phone calls

> **Situations/functions**
> Dealing with incoming hotel phone calls
> Polite greetings
>
> **Structures**
> Questions and requests:
> *Can/Could, I'd like to*
>
> Reception equipment, customer and guest titles

■ Starter

Tell students to look at the photographs. Check that they know what job the people are doing, and write *receptionist* on the board. Ask students to name four pieces of equipment in the photograph of the reception area. Check if any of your students are working in hotels at the moment, or if any of them have had work placements in hotels. If so, ask if they worked on reception and what equipment they used. Encourage use of English, although difficult at this stage. Pick out key words from student input, translate into English, and write on the board.

Answers

printer, computer screen, keyboard (and mouse), credit card machine

■ Listening *Taking phone calls*

Pre-teach unfamiliar vocabulary from New words to use on page 5. You could ask the stronger students to mime, explain in English, point to pictures, or translate into their own language. If necessary, give students a few minutes to check meanings in the Wordlist on page 97 of their books.

1 Tell students to read exercise 1. Check all students know the numbers 0–9. Play the recording and ask them to tick the correct answers. Play the calls again one by one and check their answers.

Answers

1 Mr Phillips   2 329   3 Rio Parthenon   4 James

Check students know how to say room numbers in English (*329 = three-two-nine*), and how to say *0* (*502 = five-oh-two*). Write more room numbers on the board and practise saying them. Keep to three-digit numbers at this stage; numbers 10–1000 are practised in Unit 2.

2 Draw students' attention to the words in the box. Ask them to identify the calls in which the words appear, and play the recording. Check their answers. Then play the calls again and ask them to write the receptionists' words in the gaps as they listen.

Answers

1 speaking	3 connect	5 through
2 help	4 calling	6 Can

Ask students to turn to the Listening script on page 66. In pairs, students practise reading the dialogues, swapping roles. Encourage a wide range of intonation to sound polite. Make a note of any problem areas, and practise chorally and individually. When students have practised enough, you could ask them to close their books and improvise the dialogues from memory. Write these prompts on the board if necessary:

Call 1: help you / room reservation / name
Call 2: room 329 / connect you
Call 3: parking space / reservations / through
Call 4: double room / tonight / name

Suggest some students perform the dialogues in front of the class.

■ Language study

Expressions to learn

Ask students to read the expressions aloud, and check pronunciation and intonation. Point out that if the expression is followed by **C**, it will usually be spoken by a *customer*; if it is followed by **S**, it will usually be spoken by a member of *staff*. Ask them to learn the expressions for homework.

New words to use

Ask students to check any words that are still unfamiliar in the Wordlist. Tell them to close their books, then elicit the words from them around the class:

Mr Horrowitz phoned to .... a room.
Another word for **to book***?*
The line is .... when you are speaking to a caller.
The boss of the hotel?
Where you put your car?
Not today?

Check pronunciation. Ask students to learn the new words for homework.

Structures to practise

Can/Could, I'd like to

3   Write on the board the target structures: *Can I have your name?* / *Could I reserve a parking space?* Point out both *Can* and *Could* are used for requests (*Could* is generally considered more polite), and *Can* is also used for offers: *Can I help you?* Draw students' attention to the example and explain that they have to write complete sentences from the prompts. Tell them to check their answers in pairs. Go over the answers with the whole class. Point out we often add *please* at the end of the sentence when making a request. An exception is *Can I help you?* This is an offer and does not need *please*.

Answers

1 Could I reserve a parking space?	4 Can I have your name?
2 Can I help you?	5 Could I speak to Miss Jennifer Diaz?
3 Can I make a room reservation?	6 Can I book a double room?

4   Write the target structure *I'd like to* on the board. Point out this is a polite way of saying *I want to*. Ask students to write the exercise, matching *I'd like to* with one of the four verbs plus one of the nouns 1–4. Let students compare their answers in pairs. Go over the answers with the whole class.

Answers

1 I'd like to speak to the manager.	3 I'd like to make a reservation.
2 I'd like to book a single room.	4 I'd like to reserve a parking space.

■ Listening *Taking messages*

Remind students that in the first Listening they practised taking phone calls. Elicit what they would do in reception if a line is busy or the person wanted is not in their room. Write *take a message* on the board.

5   Draw students' attention to the words in the box. If necessary, explain *ten o'clock* and *two o'clock* by drawing a simple clock face showing these times on the board. They may know the word *meeting*, but can check it in the Wordlist if necessary. Tell them they will hear someone talking to a hotel receptionist on the phone. Ask them to complete the information on the message pad as they listen, and play the recording. Alternatively, tell them to predict where the words will appear on the message pad, and that each word is used once. Play the recording and let students check their answers.

Answers

Message for: Mr Wollmann	Event: meeting
Room number: 502	Day: tomorrow
Caller: Mr Schmidt	Time: ten o'clock

6   Ask students to read the sentences, which are the same telephone dialogue but in the incorrect order. Tell them to put the sentences in the correct order by numbering the boxes 1–5. Play the recording and let students check their answers. Play the recording again and ask them to complete the sentences as they listen. Alternatively, tell them to predict where the words from exercise 5 will appear. Play the recording again and let them check their answers. Ask students to turn to the Listening script on page 66. Students practise reading the dialogue in pairs, swapping roles. Go around and monitor their performance, helping where necessary. If the students have difficulty with pronunciation and intonation, make a note of any problem areas and model these again afterwards, with students repeating after you. When the students have practised enough, you could ask them to improvise the dialogue from memory.

■ Activity

Tell students they are going to practise taking phone calls, and asking for and giving information. With weaker students, revise important words and information needed. Divide the class into pairs, Student A and Student B, and sit them back-to-back. Direct them to the correct page for each role, reminding them not to look at each other's information. When they have read the information, ask Student A to start the first call by answering the phone: *Good afternoon, Hotel Canaria. How can I help you?* Encourage them to note down the important information. When all six phone calls have finished, tell students to turn around and check the accuracy of the information they noted down. Go over general problems with the class, particularly any expressions you heard that were impolite or inappropriate.

More words to use

Ask students to read the words aloud and check pronunciation of the more difficult items: *Mrs, Ms, Dr*. Point out the titles (except *Dr*) are always used with the person's family name in spoken English, not on their own: *Good morning, Mr Schmidt*. Remind students of the use of *sir* and *madam*, which can be used without the person's family name: *Certainly, sir*. Ask students to learn the words for homework.

2 Giving information

- **Situations/functions**
  Identifying yourself: *My name's ... / I'm ...*
- **Structures**
  Is there?/Are there?, There is/There are, There isn't/There aren't
- **Numbers**
  0–1000

Revision of Unit 1

Expressions to learn

Elicit expressions by giving prompts: *The phone rings in reception and you answer it. / Ask for a name. / The person is out. Offer to take a message*, etc. With a weaker group, you could refer them to the list of expressions, let them read them first, and then give prompts in a different order to the list.

New words to use / More words to use

It is worth spending ten minutes beforehand writing down words on individual pieces of paper, or flashcards. Give students one word each, which they do not show to anyone. Tell them to try to: explain the meaning of the word in English; give a sentence with the word in context; translate the word into their native language. This can also be done in small groups. Just one of these tasks may be suitable for some groups. Translation is probably the easiest. Recycle by collecting the flashcards in and redistributing them. Make sure you keep them for future revision.

Other revision suggestions

- Ask students to count up to *10*.
- Ask students to read room numbers from the board: *101–999*.
- Get students to practise dialogues, reading the Listening script from Unit 1.
- Tell students to do the Activity from Unit 1, working with a different partner.

Starter

Tell the class to look at the photos. Ask if students can identify the two cities (London and Sydney). Ask what other foreign cities they know or have visited. Finally, ask what foreign cities they would like to visit or work in. Draw students' attention to the eight words given in the Student's Book. Suggest they do the task individually, then check their answers.

Answers

café, taxi, bus, restaurant, waiter and *hotel* should be ticked.

Listening *Where people work*

Pre-teach potentially difficult vocabulary from New words to use. See Unit 1 for suggestions about ways of doing this. Practise pronunciation of more difficult items such as *disabled access, air-conditioning,* and *Internet access*. Not all of the items appear in the first Listening but they occur later in the unit. The concept of learning vocabulary in related words groups, or in commonly used phrases or 'chunks' rather than isolated, unconnected words is good practice. Ask students if they know any other hotel facilities, or if they have worked in places with other facilities. Explain an *à la carte* menu. (*À la carte* diners are free to choose one or more courses from a number of options.) Practise pronunciation of *à la carte* /æ lə kɑːt/.

1 Ask students to look at the photographs and at the tables with the missing information. Play the recording and ask the students to complete the tables. Play the recording again and check if all students had the correct answers.

Answers

Cumberland Hotel: London; 900 rooms; 8 floors; 1 shop
Sydney Tower Restaurant: Sydney, Australia; 200 seats; international cuisine; 1 bar

2 Tell the students that when we talk about numbers we often use *There is* and *There are*. Write them on the board. Draw their attention to the singular short form: *There's*. Students may be able to complete exercise 2 without listening again. If not, play the recording again and let them check their answers. Point out the difference between the statement, the question form, and the negative: *There is/There are; Is there?/Are there?* and *There isn't/There aren't*.

Answers

1 in	3 floors	5 Is there	7 There are
2 There are	4 There's	6 300	8 there

Ask students to turn to the Listening script on page 66. In pairs, students practise reading the dialogues. Make a note of any errors in pronunciation and intonation, and practise chorally and individually. When students have

8 | Unit 2 Giving information

practised enough, you could ask them to substitute different names and information for the two interviews and to continue practising in pairs. Suggest some students perform the dialogues with substituted information in front of the class.

- **Language study**

Expressions to learn

Ask students to read the expressions aloud and check pronunciation and intonation. Ask them to learn the expressions for homework.

New words to use

Ask students to check any words that are still unfamiliar in the Wordlist. Elicit the words from them around the class, preferably with books closed. You could also write the easier words to mime on flashcards and give them to individual students to act out in front of the class or in small groups. Make sure you keep your flashcards for future revision. Ask students to learn the new words for homework.

Structures to practise

Is there?/Are there?, There is/There are, There isn't/ There aren't

Review the target structures on the board by writing:

Is there?/Are there? for asking questions
Yes, there is./Yes, there are and *No, there isn't./No, there aren't* for giving information.

Practise the sentences in the example chorally and individually.

3   Ask students to read the information about the Plaza Hotel. Tell them to write six two-line dialogues using this information. They can use *Is there?/Are there?* to ask questions. Draw their attention to the examples. As they write, go around the class and help, correct, or make suggestions. Then ask students to practise their dialogues in pairs. Correct and model any errors.

- **Listening** *What facilities are there?*

4   Students should be familiar with the words in the list of facilities. Give them a few minutes to match the words and symbols, and to check their answers in pairs. Play the recording and let them check their answers.

Answers

1 g	3 h	5 i	7 j	9 f	11 l
2 a	4 k	6 d	8 c	10 e	12 b

5   This Listening recycles language already dealt with in the unit, except for two phrases: *change money* and *park my car*. Check comprehension and play the recording. Tell students to do the task by noting the letter of the facilities available on the list in exercise 4 as they listen. Play the recording again and let them check their answers.

Answers

l, b, c, k

Ask students to turn to the Listening script on page 66 and get them to practise reading the dialogue in pairs, swapping roles. Go around and monitor their performance, helping where necessary. If students have difficulty with pronunciation and intonation, make a note of the problem areas and model these again afterwards, with students repeating after you.

- **Activity**

Tell students they are going to practise giving information about hotel facilities, face-to-face. If necessary, revise important words and information needed. Divide the class into pairs, Student A and Student B. Direct them to the correct page for each role, reminding them not to look at the other student's information. When they have read the information, ask Student A to start by asking about the Manor Hotel, Melbourne: *Excuse me, is there a restaurant?* Remind them they should write *yes* or *no*, depending on Student B's answer. When Student A has all the information required, tell them to swap roles and Student B asks about facilities in the Hyatt Hotel Barcelona, completing the information. Go around the class, helping students where necessary. When they have finished, tell students to turn around and compare the information they completed.

More words to use

Before reading the list, practise potentially difficult numbers: *15, 40* (written *forty*), *50, 100/1000* (*a hundred/ a thousand* rather than *one hundred/one thousand*). Read the numbers aloud and ask students to repeat after you. Ask students to respond chorally to random numbers you write on the board. Contrast the stress in numbers with similar sounds: *thirteen, thirty*, etc. If the class is confident, show them how *20–99* are formed. You could also point out the *and* in 101 (*a hundred **and** one*), etc.

3 Taking room reservations

→ **Situations/functions**
Handling enquiries
Taking reservations
Confirming by email

→ **Structures**
Do/Does
Prepositions of time: *at, on, in, from … to*

→ **Days of the week**

■ **Revision of Unit 2**

Expressions to learn

Introduce yourself: *Good morning. My name's …*
Ask students to introduce themselves. Also informally:
Hello, I'm …

Write four or five hotel facilities on the board: *bar* (✓✓), *satellite TV* (✓), *Internet access* (✓), *air-conditioning* (✓), *swimming pool* (✗), *disabled access* (✗).

Model one set of question and answer:

A *Is there a bar in the hotel?*
B *Yes. There are two bars.*

Nominate students to ask and answer with the other facilities.

Write *à la carte* on the board. Ask if anyone can explain what it means. (See the explanation in the notes for Unit 2.)

New words to use

Unit 2 covered a difficult new area of vocabulary (hotel facilities) which will occur repeatedly throughout the coursebook. It is worth spending a little time beforehand preparing flashcards, as in the revision suggestions for Unit 1. Miming the facilities or dividing the class into groups to test each other by giving translations are useful ways of making sure you have a positive start to the lesson.

More words to use

Give students a time limit to look over the list of numbers on page 7 of the Student's Book. Remind them of the few exceptions: *15, 50, 100, 101*. Write random numbers on the board, nominating students to read them aloud.

Other revision suggestions

- Get students to practise dialogues, reading the Listening script from Unit 2.
- Tell students to do the Activity section from Unit 2, working with a different partner.

■ **Starter**

Check if there is anybody with experience of working as a receptionist or reservations clerk in your class. If so, ask what kind of questions customers ask over the phone, and what information the receptionist or reservation clerk needs to know. Tell students to look at the pictures of the rooms and identify the different types. Check that everyone labels the photos correctly.

Answers

| 1 b | 2 c | 3 d | 4 a |

■ **Listening** *Taking a reservation*

Pre-teach potentially difficult vocabulary from New words to use. If necessary, give students a few minutes to check any unfamiliar words in the Wordlist.

1 Tell them they are going to hear a phone call of Mrs Morell making a room reservation. Ask if students can predict any of the expressions in the dialogue. Write their predictions on the board. Ask them to see if their predictions were correct as they listen, and play the recording. Tell them to read questions 1–5. Ask them to circle the answers *Yes* or *No*, and play the recording. Check the answers around the class.

Answers

| 1 No | 2 Yes | 3 Yes | 4 No | 5 Yes |

2 Tell students to look at the picture of the computer screen, and point out that it is part of the New reservation screen from the Fidelio bookings system which is used worldwide by hotels. Ask if any of your students are familiar with Fidelio. Explain the titles of the white boxes, and that for telephone numbers we usually read *0* as *oh* rather than *zero*. Ask students to complete the reservation information as they listen, and play the recording. Check the answers around the class.

Answers

Nights: 2   Contact number: 07780 161236
Adults: 2   Contact name: Julia Morell
Room type: double

Ask students to turn to the Listening script on page 66. Model and repeat difficult sentences and phrases, and get students to repeat after you chorally and individually. Students practise reading the dialogue in pairs, swapping roles. Try this with students sitting back-to-back and talking over their shoulders to make the telephone scenario more realistic. Alternatively, the activity could be transferred to the language or computer lab. Go around and monitor their performance, helping where necessary. If the students have difficulty with pronunciation and intonation, make a note of the problem areas and model these again afterwards, with students repeating after you. Suggest some students perform the dialogue in front of the class.

■ Language study

Expressions to learn

Ask students to read the expressions aloud and check pronunciation and intonation. They have met all the expressions before in the first Listening so there shouldn't be any problem with comprehension. Ask them to learn the expressions for homework.

New words to use

Revise these with a quick word game around the class. Ask students to give you a synonym, an opposite (antonym), or an associated word to make up a pair:

adjoining – rooms
arrive – depart
bath – shower
breakfast – lunch, dinner
departure – arrival
family – children, mother, father
children – parents (help with this new word if necessary)

Ask students to learn the new words for homework.

Structures to practise

Do, Does

Forming questions with the verb *do* is an important new area for students. Draw their attention to the example sentences. Explain that most questions in the Present Simple are formed in this way. Emphasize that only third person subjects (*he/she/it*) take *does*. Point out the positive and negative short answers, again emphasizing that only third person subjects take *does/doesn't*.

3 Write on the board: ***Do you serve*** lunch? Ask students for alternative endings to the question. Tell students to close their books and elicit questions around the class giving prompts like *dinner*. Nominate students to respond.

Draw students' attention to the next example in the book:

A *Do you serve dinner?*
B *Yes, we **do**./No, we **don't**.*

Ask students to practise questions and answers with a partner, swapping roles.

Prepositions of time

Check students know the days of the week and the months of the year. For the months you may need to refer ahead to page 11 of the Student's Book. Also check students know how to say simple times: *09.00 (nine), 10.00 (ten), 11.30 (eleven thirty)*. Ask students to read the examples of the prepositions of time. Point out the different uses:

on for days and dates
at for clock times and particular periods like the weekend
in for periods of time, months, a certain year, seasons, and parts of the day. The exception is *at night*.
from ... to with clock times, days, dates, years, and months.

Practise around the class by giving a day, month, time, etc. Ask students to give the preposition and repeat the word or phrase.

4 Check that students know the meaning of the verbs: *close, open, start, serve*. Draw students' attention to the example sentences. Relate the example sentences to the prompts in 1 and, if necessary, model it as another example using one of the stronger students. Ask students to write sentences for prompts 2–6, then ask around the class for their answers. Write correct pairs of sentences on the board and let the class check their sentences with those on the board.

Answers

1 Does the restaurant close on Sundays?
  No, it closes on Mondays.

2 Does the exchange bureau open at 9.00?
  Yes, it does.

3 Do the shops close at the weekend?
  No, they don't.

4 Does the summer season start in July?
  No, it starts in June.

5 Do you serve tea in the afternoon?
  Yes, we do.

6 Does the hotel serve dinner from 7.00 to 11.00?
  No, it serves dinner from 7.00 to 10.00.

■ Listening *Checking and confirming*

5 Tell students they are going to hear a voicemail message of a room reservation. They may be unfamiliar with dates (to be covered in more detail in Unit 4). If so, write *18th* and *23rd* on the board and get students to repeat after you: *the eighteenth, the twenty-third*. Ask students if they can predict the correct order of the message. Before playing the recording, remind students that two of the sentences begin with *I'd like*. Play the recording and let students check their answers. If necessary, play the recording again sentence by sentence and check that all students have the correct order.

Answers

The correct order is 6, 4, 2, 5, 1, 3

6 Draw students' attention to the six words in the box and check they understand them. Point out the email greeting: *Dear Mr Dickson*. Also, point out how the email is finished: *Regards Trudi Schmidt*, plus her job area *Reservations*. *Best/Kind regards* are alternative endings. Ask students to complete the email, and then check their answers in pairs. Read the completed email aloud for students to check their answers.

Answers

1 confirm	3 reserved	5 table
2 twin	4 car park	6 7.30

■ Activity

Tell students they are going to practise taking room reservations over the phone. If necessary, revise important words and information needed. Divide the class into pairs, Student A and Student B, and sit them back-to-back. Direct them to the correct page for each role, reminding them not to look at the other student's information. When they have read the information, ask Student A to start the first call by answering the phone: *Good morning, Sonotel Hotel. Can I help you?* Go around the class, helping where necessary. Encourage students to note down important information. When both phone calls have finished, tell students to turn around and check the accuracy of the information they noted down. Go over general problems with the class, particularly any expressions you heard that were impolite or inappropriate.

More words to use

Ask the class to recite the days of the week with their books closed. Model and repeat any pronunciation difficulties. Read the family members aloud with students repeating after you. Tell them to check any unfamiliar words in the Wordlist. The email abbreviations are there for reference. They will probably already know some of these, but you could point out *attn*, when you have a company email address but you want your message to be read by a particular person: *Attn. Miranda di Caprio*. Also, *re* for referring to the subject of an email or a past email: *Re your email yesterday*. If students are confident enough at spelling, this might be a good opportunity to look at how we read email addresses aloud:

@ = *at*
. = *dot*
.com and .co are read as two syllables = *dot com* and *dot co*
/ = *(forward) slash*
\ = *back slash*
- = *hyphen*
_ = *underscore*

Ask students to learn Expressions to learn, New words to use, and More words to use for homework.

Unit 3 Taking room reservations

4 Taking restaurant bookings

- **Situations/functions**
  Talking about times and availability
- **Structures**
  Adverbs of frequency:
  always, *often*, *sometimes*, *rarely*, *never*
- **Dates, times**

Revision of Unit 3

Expressions to learn

Write the following on the board as a gapfill exercise. Tell students to complete it with their books closed.

Guest:	.... book a room, please.
Receptionist:	Yes, we have a double room .... nights is it for?
Guest:	Two nights. Tomorrow and Friday.
Receptionist:	OK. Could you .... an email to .... your reservation? Also, ... you .... a contact number?

New words to use / More words to use

Recycle as suggested in Unit 2, using flashcards. Recycle further by writing one word from each word group on the board and ask students to complete the group. Word groups in Unit 3 are: room types, family members, meals, days of the week.

Other revision suggestions

- Get students to practise dialogues, reading the Listening script from Unit 3.
- Tell students to do the Activity from Unit 3, working with a different partner.

Starter

Check if any of your students work or have worked in restaurants, bars, or cafés. If so, ask about what kind of places they were, and what the working hours were. Alternatively, ask what kind of restaurants, bars, or cafés they like to go to. Give students a few minutes to look at the puzzle then check the answers in class.

Answers

> pizzeria, café, bar
> brasserie = a type of café bar that serves food, common in continental Europe.

Listening *I'd like to book a table*

Most of the words in this Listening will be familiar to students. Pre-teach: *fully booked*, *cancellation* and the difference between *a.m.* and *p.m.* (*a.m.* = midnight to 11.59 in the morning; *p.m.* = midday to 11.59 at night).

1 Tell students they are going to hear a phone dialogue between a customer, Mrs Kruger, who wants to book a table, and a restaurant manager. Draw their attention to the sentences in exercise 1 and ask them to mark *true* or *false* as they listen. Play the recording, pausing after each *true/false* piece of information if necessary. Play the recording again so that students can check their answers.

Answers

| 1 false | 2 true | 3 false | 4 true | 5 false |

2 Draw students' attention to sentences 1–5. Ask students to complete the answers as they listen, and play the recording a final time. Let them compare their answers in pairs. Check the answers around the class and, if necessary, read the completed sentences and ask students to repeat chorally.

Answers

1 from Tuesday, Sunday	4 from twelve, three
2 on Mondays	5 we're fully booked
3 from seven, eleven	

Ask students to match these responses to sentences a–e.

Answers

| 1 d | 2 a | 3 c | 4 e | 5 b |

Students can practise these questions and answers in pairs, swapping roles. When students can use them confidently, ask them to turn to the Listening script and practise the phone call sitting back-to-back. Check pronunciation and encourage a wide range of intonation to sound polite. Suggest one pair performs the dialogue in front of the class.

Language study

Expressions to learn

Ask students to read the expressions aloud, and check their pronunciation and intonation. They have recently used them all while practising with the Listening script. Ask students to learn the expressions for homework.

New words to use

Ask the class to read the words aloud. They will have met most of them already in the first Listening. Explain *o'clock*: when the time is actually on the hour we sometimes say *one o'clock, two o'clock* rather than just *one* or *two*. Ask students to learn the new words for homework.

Structures to practise

Dates

If necessary, revise the months of the year. Read them aloud while students repeat after you. Ask them to say the months in order around the class. Now ask students to look at the list of Ordinal numbers on page 110 of the Student's Book. Explain the irregularity of *1st, 2nd, 3rd*, and the *-ieth* of *20th, 30th*, etc. and practise pronunciation. Test students by writing some dates on the board, as we would usually write them: *8 March, 1 April, 22 July*. Listen for **the** *eighth* **of** *March*, etc.

3   In this exercise, the dates are written in bracketed numbers, the British way, with the day first and the month second: *5/8 is 5th August*. Point out that in US English (and in many other countries) the month is written first, so *5/8 is 8th May*. If students are confident, try doing the exercise orally around the class, making sure they are saying *the … of …* for each date. Change the dates of the exercise so everyone has a turn.

Adverbs of frequency

Draw a diagram on the board similar to that on page 76 of the Student's Book. Give some examples of things you *always, often, sometimes, rarely, never* do:
I always check my emails in the morning.
I often watch TV in the evening.
I sometimes go shopping at the weekend.
Draw students' attention to the examples in their books.

4   Ask them to make a list of things they do, using all the adverbs of frequency. Ask one of the stronger students to read aloud sentence A of the example dialogue. Reply with the first alternative: *No, I rarely … .* Repeat the procedure with a different student and read the other alternative: *Yes, I always … .* Ask students to practise exchanging information with a partner.

■ **Listening** *What time is it?*

5   Before playing the recording, revise times and numbers around the class by writing some examples on the board. Keep to *o'clock* and every quarter at this stage. Ask students to write the times next to the clock faces in their books as they listen, and play the recording. Check answers around the class.

Answers

| 1 c | 2 d | 3 a | 4 b |

6   Explain that there are different ways of saying the time. *7.05* can be read as *seven oh five* or *five past seven*; *7.15* as *a quarter past seven*; *7.30* as *half past seven*. Give students some practice with saying the time using the word *past*. Do the same with *to* the hour. Ask the students to write the times in each sign as they listen, and play the recording. Let them compare their answers in pairs. Ask them to read their answers around the class, and ask for the alternative version as well.

Answers

a 11.05	d 7.15
b 5.30	e 1.10
c 8.45	f 06.35

7   Ask students to turn to the Listening script for exercise 6 on page 67. Read some of the questions. Ask them how questions about time begin. If they are not sure, tell them: except for *What's **the** time?*, questions about time always begin *What time …?* or *When …?* Each prompt in exercise 7 forms the basis for a question and answer. Draw students' attention to the example, and the question and answer made from the prompt. Ask the students to write questions and answers for prompts 1–6 and check their answers in pairs. Check the answers around the class.

Answers

1 When does the restaurant open for lunch?
   From 12.15 to 3 p.m. / From a quarter past twelve to three o'clock.
2 What time does my flight leave?
   At 18.20. / At twenty past six in the evening.
3 When does the group arrive from Russia?
   At 6.45 p.m. / At a quarter to seven in the evening.
4 What time does the exchange bureau open?
   At 8 a.m. / At 8 o'clock in the morning.
5 What time does the train leave?
   At 14.50. / At ten to three in the afternoon.
6 When does the fitness centre close?
   At 10.30 p.m. / At half past ten in the evening.

Ask students to practise the dialogues in pairs, taking it in turns to ask and answer. Monitor pronunciation and intonation, making a note of any mistakes to correct afterwards.

- **Activity**

Tell students they are going to practise taking restaurant reservations over the phone. If necessary, revise important words and information needed. Divide the class into pairs, Student A and Student B, and sit them back-to-back. Direct them to the correct page for each role, reminding them not to look at the other student's information. Draw their attention to the example calls to help give an idea of what they are expected to do. When they have read the information, ask Student A to start the first call by answering the phone: *Good evening,* (name of chosen restaurant). *Can I help you?* Go around the class, helping students where necessary. Encourage them to note down the important information. When all the reservations have been made, tell students to turn around and check the accuracy of the information they noted down. Go over general problems with the class, particularly any expressions you heard that were impolite or inappropriate.

More words to use

Since this has already been covered in this unit (and perhaps in Unit 3), test students' pronunciation of the months with their books closed. If necessary, ask them to learn the words for homework.

5 Giving polite explanations

··▷ **Situations/functions**
Turning down reservations:
I'm sorry/I'm afraid/Unfortunately
Written apologies

··▷ **Structures**
Short forms: *be*, *do*, *can*

··▷ **Times of day**

■ Revision of Unit 4

Expressions to learn

Elicit expressions by getting students to do the following: Make a reservation. / Ask what days the restaurant is open. / Say you are open from Tuesday to Sunday. / Ask what time they serve dinner. / Say you sometimes have cancellations. / Say you have a table on the 23rd. / Say Friday the 23rd is fine.

New words to use

Recycle as suggested in Unit 2, using flashcards.

More words to use

Ask students to recite the months of the year chorally.

Other revision suggestions

- Write times and dates on the board, and ask students to read them aloud.
- Write the five frequency adverbs on the board (*always, often, sometimes, rarely, never*) and ask students to say sentences about themselves using them.
- Tell students to do the Activity from Unit 4, working with a different partner.

■ Starter

Tell students to look at the pictures. Ask them what parts of the hotel they can see. Ask students what other rooms or parts of a hotel they can name. List them on the board.

Answers

| reception, car park, restaurant, bathroom |

■ Listening *Making apologies*

Pre-teach potentially difficult vocabulary from New words to use. If necessary, give students a few minutes to check any unfamiliar vocabulary in the Wordlist. Ask if anyone in the class has had to apologize for a problem in a work situation. If so, ask how easy or difficult they found it and what words they used.

1 Tell students they are going to hear eight short dialogues. Ask them to identify which place the dialogues refer to. Play the recording and then check their answers.

Answers

1 hotel	3 hotel	5 car park	7 hotel
2 restaurant	4 restaurant	6 restaurant	8 hotel

2 Draw students' attention to sentences 1–8. Ask them to predict the missing words. Play the recording again and let them check their answers.

Answers

1 hotel's	3 booked	5 full	7 afraid
2 closed	4 sorry	6 open	8 sorry

Point out the way in which we make apologies, by starting the sentence with *I'm sorry, I'm afraid, Unfortunately*. Ask students to turn to the Listening script on page 67. Model difficult and important phrases and structures, and get students to repeat them chorally and individually. Students practise reading the short dialogues in pairs, swapping roles. Go around and monitor their performance, helping where necessary. If students have difficulty with pronunciation or intonation, make a note of the problem areas and model these again afterwards, with students repeating after you.

■ Language study

Expressions to learn

Ask students to read the expressions aloud and check pronunciation and intonation. Ask them to learn the expressions for homework.

New words to use

Ask students to read the words aloud and check pronunciation. Tell them to check any unfamiliar words in the Wordlist. Ask the class to learn the new words for homework.

Structures to practise

Present Simple (short forms)

Draw students' attention to the short forms used in Expressions to learn. Explain that in spoken English we usually use short forms rather than full forms: *I'm* rather than *I am*. This is because they are easier and quicker to say. Read the examples of *be* and *have* aloud.

Write tables of the short forms of *be* and *have* on the board, both positive and negative forms. Ask students to help you complete them. Follow the same procedure with the negative examples of *do* and *can*.

3 Read sentences 1–9 aloud and check comprehension. Ask students to rewrite the sentences using the short forms. Point out that there is more than one verb in sentences 1, 3, 6, 8, and 9. Go over the answers with the whole class.

Answers

1 I'm sorry, we're closed	6 She can't, She isn't
2 We don't have	7 He doesn't
3 I'm afraid I can't	8 I'm sorry, we don't have
4 He's	9 Here's, You're
5 They aren't	

Ask students to practise speaking the short forms in pairs. Check their pronunciation.

4 Read the example aloud. Draw students' attention to requests 1–5 and check their comprehension. Ask two stronger students to do number 1 as another example, if necessary. One student reads the request and the other refuses using the prompt. Make sure they use the short forms. Practise around the class several times.

Answers

1 I'm sorry,/I'm afraid/Unfortunately, we're fully booked.
2 I'm sorry,/I'm afraid/Unfortunately, the car park's full.
3 I'm sorry,/I'm afraid/Unfortunately, we're closed on Tuesdays.
4 I'm sorry,/I'm afraid/Unfortunately, there isn't an answer from 248.
5 I'm sorry,/I'm afraid/Unfortunately, we're only open in the evenings.

■ **Listening** *Written apologies*

Tell students written English is more formal than spoken English, and short forms are less commonly used. Explain that there are certain recognized phrases that they can learn and use for emails, faxes, and letters.

5 Ask students to read the written apologies. Check comprehension. Point out that *I regret* is a formal written alternative to *I'm sorry* in spoken English. Also point out that *We* is often used when speaking on behalf of an organization or company. Ask students to listen to each voicemail message and match them with the appropriate written reply by writing *a–e*. Play the recording, pausing after each message if necessary. Check the answers with the whole class.

Answers

| 1 e | 2 a | 3 d | 4 c | 5 b |

6 Ask students to read the email. Check comprehension. Write on the board the four tasks in the email reply: *confirm the room booking; apologize that the bathrooms only have showers; apologize because there aren't any parking spaces until Wednesday; confirm the table booking.* Tell the students to work in pairs to write the email reply. Go around the class checking and correcting their writing. Elicit the four sentences needed and write a model email on the board.

Model answer

Dear Mr Rogers
We confirm your reservation of two adjoining double rooms, one with twin beds, for five nights from Monday 28th August. We regret that the bathrooms only have showers.
We also regret that there aren't any parking spaces available in the hotel car park until Wednesday 30th August.
A table for four is reserved in the restaurant for you at 7.00pm.
Best regards

■ **Activity**

Tell students they are going to practise giving polite explanations over the phone. If necessary, revise important words and information needed. Divide the class into pairs, Student A and Student B, and sit them back-to-back. Direct them to the correct page for each role, reminding them not to look at the other student's information. Draw their attention to the example calls to help give an idea of what they are expected to do. When they have read the information, ask Student B to start the first call by answering the phone: *Hello, Hotel Palazzo. How can I help you?* Go around the class, helping students where necessary. Encourage them to note down the important information. When all four phone calls have finished, tell students to turn around and check the accuracy of the information they noted down. Go over general problems with the class, particularly any expressions you heard that were impolite or inappropriate.

More words to use

Ask the students to read the words aloud and check pronunciation. Ask them to learn the words for homework.

6 Receiving guests

- **Situations/functions**
  Polite requests and queries
  Asking and explaining where places are
- **Structures**
  Possessive adjectives:
  my, your, his, her, our, your, their
- **Seasons and special occasions**

Revision of Unit 5

Expressions to learn

Ask students to give the spoken apology forms *I'm sorry/ I'm afraid/Unfortunately* in sentences in response to your prompts:

*The hotel's fully booked that weekend.
The restaurant's closed on Sundays.
The hotel's full on Tuesday.
There isn't anything left for tomorrow.
The restaurant's only open in the evenings.
The bathroom only has a shower.*

As follow-up, and in contrast, ask students to give you the written apology form for these sentences.

New words to use / More words to use

Recycle as suggested in Unit 2, using flashcards.

Other revision suggestions

- Revise short forms by giving students the long form and asking them for the short form.
- Get students to practise dialogues, reading the first Listening script from Unit 5.
- Tell students to do the Activity from Unit 5, working with a different partner.

Starter

Check students know the name of the place where hotel guests check in (reception). Ask about their experience of work or work placement in a hotel reception; or receptions they may have visited which were impressive or unimpressive. Ask students to tick the items they can see in the photograph of the hotel reception.

Answers

Only *receptionist, reception desk, luggage,* and *key card* should be ticked.

Listening *Checking into a hotel*

Pre-teach potentially difficult vocabulary from New words to use. See Unit 1 for suggestions about ways of doing this. Practise pronunciation of difficult items such as *home address, key card, lounge, luggage,* and *registration card*.

1 Ask students to look at the hotel registration card. Check they know which four pieces of information they must listen for in the recording. Ask them to complete the registration card as they listen, and play the recording. Check their answers around the class.

Answers

Mr Rodrigues, 10th June, 12th June, 361

2 Ask students to look at sentences 1–6 in pairs and see if they can predict the missing words. Play the recording again and let students check and correct their answers.

Answers

1 afternoon, help	3 fill	5 could, your
2 My	4 my	6 help, your

Tell students to turn to the Listening script on page 67. Get them to practise reading the dialogue in pairs, swapping roles. Go around the class and monitor their performance. Make a note of any errors in pronunciation and intonation, and model these afterwards, with students repeating after you. You could ask stronger students to substitute the key information with different items and to continue practising in pairs. Suggest one pair of students performs the dialogue in front of the class.

Language study

Expressions to learn

Ask students to read the expressions aloud, and check their pronunciation and intonation. Ask them to learn the expressions for homework.

New words to use

Ask students to read the list of words aloud and check pronunciation. Tell them to check any unfamiliar words in the Wordlist. Ask students to learn the new words for homework.

Structures to practise

Possessive adjectives

Pick out examples of target structures from the first Listening script and write them on the board: *my name, your passport, your room number*. Read the other forms, which are given in the Student's Book. Give examples of these forms by pointing around the class, using vocabulary the students will know: *her bag, his shoes, its door* (the classroom's), *our classroom, your teacher, their books*. Ask students to do the same. Point out that the possessive adjective *its* doesn't have an apostrophe. *It's* is the short form of *it is*. If it is likely to be a problem area for your students, also point out that in English nouns do not have genders. *His* and *her* refer to the gender of the person who possesses the item. The possessive adjective remains the same whether the word it refers to is singular or plural.

3 Ask students to read sentences 1–6 and check comprehension. Tell them to complete the sentences with one of the possessive adjectives. Check their answers around the class.

Answers

| 1 my | 2 your | 3 our | 4 his | 5 her | 6 their |

■ **Listening** *Where is it?*

Draw students' attention to the preposition diagrams for *in, on, next to, opposite,* and *behind*. Give them more practice with examples of objects and people in the classroom.

4 Ask students to read the names of the five places they have to mark on the hotel plan. Check comprehension. Ask them to mark the places on the plan as they listen, and play the recording. Alternatively, you could ask weaker students to number the order in which they hear the places occur: 1 *bar*, 2 *fitness centre*, 3 *lounge*, 4 *hair salon*, 5 *sauna*. Play the recording again and let them check and correct their answers.

Answers

| 1 b | 2 d | 3 a | 4 c | 5 e |

Ask students to turn to the Listening script on pages 67–8 and get them to practise reading the dialogues in pairs, swapping roles. Go around and monitor their performance, helping where necessary. If students have difficulty with pronunciation and intonation, make a note of problem areas and model these again afterwards, with students repeating after you.

5 Tell students to continue practising in pairs, looking at the hotel plan and asking for and giving directions. Suggest some pairs of students practise their questions and answers in front of the class.

■ **Activity**

Tell students they are going to practise checking in a hotel guest. If necessary, revise important words and information needed. Divide the class into pairs, Student A and Student B. Direct them to the correct page for each role, reminding them not to look at the other student's information. When they have read the information, ask Student A (as the receptionist) to start by greeting the guests: *Good morning. How can I help you?* Remind students the roles are then reversed, and Student A plays the part of two guests checking in. Go around the class, helping students where necessary. Encourage them to note down the important information. When the four role-plays have finished, tell students to check the accuracy of the information they noted down. Go over any general problems with the class, particularly any expressions you heard that were impolite or inappropriate.

More words to use

Ask students to read the seasons of the year and to learn them for homework.

Read the special occasions list aloud and explain where necessary. If appropriate, ask students about other special occasions and add to the list:

Christmas – Christian festival celebrating the birth of Christ. Symbols of decorated tree and homes, gifts, and festive food.

Easter – Christian festival celebrating Christ's resurrection from the dead. Symbol of chocolate eggs.

New Year – International festival marking the beginning of a new calendar year. Often interpreted differently, and at different times of the year, according to country and religion.

Diwali – Hindu festival of light. Symbols of lamps, candles, and sweets.

Ramadan – Muslim, annual, one-month fast period between sunrise and sunset.

7 Serving in the bar

- **Situations/functions**
  Asking what people would like to drink
  Asking how they would like to pay
- **Structures**
  Polite requests and offers:
  Can, Could, Shall, Would you like?
- **Names and types of drinks**

■ Revision of Unit 6

Expressions to learn
Write the sentences below on the board as a gapfill exercise. Give students the following words to use: *fill in, key card, reserve, third, table, number, check in, registration card, dinner.* Tell students to complete the sentences with their books closed.

Guest: I'd like to ...., please.
Receptionist: Could you please ....
this ....?
Here's your .... for your room.
Your room ....'s 361. It's on the .... floor.
Would you like to have .... in the restaurant?
Guest: Yes, please. Can you .... me a .... for two at 8 o'clock?

New words to use / More words to use
Recycle as suggested in Unit 2, using flashcards.

Possessive adjectives
Give examples of possessive adjectives followed by nouns using items in the room: *their books, her pen, my bag.* Elicit more examples from the students by pointing, or using gestures, or using pictures.

Prepositions
Write *Where's the ...?* on the board. Give students examples of questions and answers using *in, on, next to, opposite,* and *behind.* Ask students to make similar questions and answers using the hotel plan from Unit 6.

Other revision suggestions
- Ask students to recite the seasons of the year.
- Get students to practise dialogues, reading the Listening script from Unit 6.
- Tell students to do the Activity from Unit 6, working with a different partner.

■ Starter
Check if any of your students have worked in a bar. If so, ask what kind of places they were, and the most popular drinks they served. Alternatively, ask what kind of bars or cafés students like to go to, and what they usually order to drink. Tell students to look at the pictures of all the bottles and cans of drink. Read the names on the labels aloud and ask students to repeat after you. Explain the four different categories of drinks: *spirits* = British English (*liquor* /ˈlɪkə/ = US English); *soft drinks/mixers* = non-alcoholic drinks like cola, lemonade, etc. that can be mixed with alcohol or drunk alone. Ask students to tell you which category the drinks belong in.

Answers

beer:	Leffe, San Miguel, Guinness
wine:	Yellow Tail Chardonnay, Campo Viejo Rioja
spirits:	Remy Martin brandy, Stolichnaya vodka, Gordon's gin, Bell's whisky
soft drinks /mixers	Badoit water, Spa water, Schweppes lemonade, Schweppes tonic water

■ Listening *What can I get you?*
Check students know what a cocktail is (a mixed drink with at least one spirit in it). Ask what else a bar server might put in a gin and tonic (ice and lemon).

1 Tell students they have to write down what the four people in the bar order to drink. Play the recording. Ask students to compare answers in pairs. Play the recording again, and let students check and correct their answers. Go over the answers with the whole class.

Answers

| 1 Guinness | 3 Margarita |
| 2 gin and tonic | 4 San Miguel |

2 Ask students to read questions 1–5. Stronger students will probably be able to predict the answers. Ask them to answer the questions, or check and correct their predictions in pairs as they listen, and play the recording. Check the answers orally around the class, modelling the pronunciation of any difficult words or phrases.

Answers

| 1 in the hotel bar | 3 bottled beer | 5 (in) cash |
| 2 a cocktail | 4 ice and lemon | |

Language study

Expressions to learn
Ask students to read the expressions aloud, and check their pronunciation and intonation. Ask them to learn the expressions for homework.

New words to use
Ask the class to read the words aloud and check their pronunciation. Explain *soda* (carbonated water often served from a siphon with whisky). Tell them to check any unfamiliar words in the Wordlist. Ask students to learn the new words for homework.

Structures to practise

Requests and offers
Read through the examples with the students. Point out that hotel and restaurant employees should always use these polite forms when talking to guests.

3 Ask students to read the four replies and, in pairs, match each one with an example question. Check their answers and ask students to practise the short dialogues in pairs. Listen for polite intonation. Model the phrases and ask students to repeat after you, if necessary.

Answers

1 Shall I charge this to your room?	3 Can I have your key card?
2 Could I have a beer?	4 Would you like ice?

Adjectives
Revise the word groups given in the Student's Book. You may want to add that wine can also be *rosé*. With their books closed, test students by matching the nouns and adjectives: *red – wine, bottled – beer*, etc.

4 Ask students to read the example. Ask them to practise asking questions with a partner to find out exactly what the customers want in requests 1–6. Tell them they should begin their questions with *Would you like?*

Model answers

1 Would you like a double or a single?	4 Would you like ice and lemon?
2 Would you like sparkling or still?	5 Would you like draught or bottled?
3 Would you like dry or medium-dry?	6 Would you like a double or a single?

Ask students to practise the dialogues in pairs, swapping roles. Monitor pronunciation and intonation. Model and ask students to repeat after you if necessary.

Listening *How much is that?*

The Student's Book uses the euro but you could substitute the currency of the students' own country by converting the prices into equivalent amounts.

5 Ask students to look at the bar tariff and check they know the names of the drinks. Tell them *Bacardi* is a kind of *rum*. Explain they should listen to the recording and note down the drinks the five people order, and whether they are large or small measures. Point out that if the customer doesn't specify large or small, the server usually assumes they require a small measure. Play the recording. Ask students in pairs to calculate how much each customer is charged. Play the recording again, and check the answers around the class.

Answers

1 €19	2 €8	3 €28	4 €29	5 €25

6 Nominate two students to read the example dialogue aloud. One is the server and the other a customer. Ask students to work in pairs and write three new dialogues, taking orders for drinks and asking for payment, using the example as a model.

Go around the class monitoring and helping where necessary. Suggest some pairs perform one of their new dialogues in front of the class.

Activity
Tell students they are going to practise serving in the bar. If necessary, revise important words and information needed. Divide the class into pairs, Student A and Student B. Draw their attention to the example dialogue to help give an idea of what they are expected to do. When they have read the information, ask Student A to start (as the customer) by ordering drinks: *Could I have…?* Remind students the roles are then reversed and Student A plays the part of the server. Go around the class, helping students where necessary. When they have finished, go over general problems with the class, particularly any expressions you heard that were impolite or inappropriate.

More words to use
Ask students to repeat after you as you read through the different groups. Tell them to learn the lists for homework.

8 Instructions

- **Situations/functions**
  Asking how to do things
  Explaining how to do things
- **Structures**
  Verbs for giving instructions
  Sequence markers: *first, next, then, finally*
- **Names of cocktails and liqueurs**

■ Revision of Unit 7

Expressions to learn

Write the sentences below on the board, and ask students to fill in the gaps. If they are confident, they can do this exercise orally.

Good evening. What can I .... you?
.... you .... draught or bottled beer?
Would you like .... and .... in your gin and tonic?
.... I charge this to your room?
No thanks. I'll pay ....

New words to use / More words to use

Draw a spidergram or mind map on the board, starting from the word *DRINKS*. Ask students to suggest different types of wine, beer, spirits, and water, and add them to the spidergram. Then ask them to suggest different measures and mixers.

Other revision suggestions

- Get students to practise making offers. Elicit *Would you like ice and lemon?* by saying to one student: *Ask another student if he or she would like ice and lemon.* Continue using requests from Unit 7, Structures to practise, exercise 4.
- Tell students to do the Activity from Unit 7, working with a different partner.

■ Starter

Ask if anyone in the class can mix cocktails. If so, ask which ones and how they mix them. Alternatively, ask if anyone knows the names of any cocktails and what they contain.

■ Listening *How do you make a cocktail?*

There is a lot of new vocabulary in this unit so it's best to spend some time working with the pictures before playing the recording. Explain that they show how to make a Margarita. Ask students to look at each picture carefully and elicit or give the names of the different items they can see: *cocktail shaker, crushed ice, measure, fresh lemon juice, lime cordial, ice cubes, salt-rimmed glass, garnish, slice of lime*. Next, try to elicit or give the verbs for the different actions involved. Some of the actions are easy to mime: *take, fill, pour, squeeze, shake, add, mix, chill, put, serve*.

1 Ask students to listen to the instructions and follow pictures 1–9. Play the recording.

2 Ask students to read the list of instructions. Check for comprehension. Ask them to match the instructions with the pictures 1–9.

Answers

1 First, take a cocktail shaker and fill it with crushed ice.
2 Next, pour in one measure of tequila.
3 Then pour in a quarter measure of triple sec.
4 Then squeeze some fresh lemon juice into the shaker.
5 Then add a dash of lime juice.
6 Shake well to mix and chill the liquids.
7 Then put some ice cubes into a salt-rimmed glass.
8 Finally, pour the Margarita into the glass and serve.
9 Garnish with a slice of lime.

Ask students to practise in pairs. One student mimes the action while the other says the instruction. Go around the class monitoring pronunciation and intonation. Note any difficulties and model the phrases afterwards, asking students to repeat after you.

■ Language study

Expressions to learn

Ask students to read the expressions aloud, and check their pronunciation and intonation. Ask them to learn the expressions for homework.

New words to use

Ask students to read the words aloud and check pronunciation. Tell them to check any unfamiliar words in the Wordlist. Ask the class to learn the new words for homework.

Structures to practise

Instructions and sequence markers

Explain that in English the base form or infinitive without *to* is used for giving instructions. Give some instructions for students to follow: *Stand up. Sit down. Pass me your book. Open the door.* Read the example in the Student's Book. (*Worcester sauce* /ˈwʊstə ˈsɔːs/ is a mildly spicy food flavouring. *Tabasco sauce* is a hot, spicy food flavouring made from peppers.) Draw students' attention to the base forms and the sequence markers.

3 Ask students to write the three short instruction paragraphs using the prompts and appropriate sequence markers. Tell them to compare their instructions with a partner. Ask some students to read their instructions to the class. Correct and model any incorrect sentences on the board.

Model answers

> 1 First, put the coffee into the cafetière. Next, boil some water. Then pour it over the coffee and fill the cafetière.
> 2 First, write the person's email address at the top of the email. Next, write the information you want to send. Finally, click on *Send*.
> 3 First, give the new guest a registration card. Next, ask the guest to fill it in. Then ask for their passport. Finally, give them the key card.

■ Listening *Can you make these drinks?*

4 Tell students they are going to hear instructions for making two well-known cocktails, a Daiquiri /ˈdækɪrɪ/ and a Manhattan. Ask students to read through the list of equipment and ingredients. Check comprehension and pronunciation. Ask students to work in pairs and try to predict which items are needed for each drink. Play the recording, and let students check their answers as they listen. Go over the answers with the whole class.

Answers

> Daiquiri: cocktail shaker, crushed ice, light rum, lemon juice, caster sugar, cocktail glass, slice of lemon
>
> Manhattan: large glass, ice, Canadian whisky, sweet vermouth, Angostura bitters, cocktail glass, slice of lemon, cherry

5 Ask students to complete the instructions using the words from exercise 4. When they have finished, play the recording again and let them check and correct their answers. Tell them they can refer to the Listening script if they are still not sure.

■ Activity

Tell students they are going to practise giving and following instructions for making cocktails. If necessary, revise important words and information needed. Divide the class into pairs, Student A and Student B. Direct them to the correct page for each role, reminding them not to look at the other student's information. When they have read the information, ask Student A to start by asking how to make a Broadway. Encourage them to note down the important information. Remind students the roles are then reversed, and Student B asks how to make a Whisky Sour. Go around the class, helping students where necessary. When both sets of instructions have been exchanged, tell students to check the accuracy of the information they noted down. Go over general problems with the class, particularly any difficulties giving instructions or using sequence markers.

More words to use

Ask students to read the words aloud and check pronunciation. Ask them to learn the names of the drinks and the fractions for homework.

9 Taking a food order

- **Situations/functions**
  Making guests feel welcome
  Taking orders for food
- **Structures**
  a/an, the
  a, some
- **Starters and main courses**

■ Revision of Unit 8

Expressions to learn

Ask students to look at the pictures in Unit 8 again and give instructions for making a Margarita.

New words to use

Recycle as suggested in Unit 2, using flashcards.

More words to use

Ask students to name the cocktails from Unit 8. Write fractions on the board and get students to say them: ¼, ½, ¾, ⅓.

Other revision suggestions:

- Ask students to give instructions how to do something using the markers: *first, next, then, finally*.
- Tell students to do the Activity from Unit 8, working with a different partner.

■ Starter

Ask students for the names of some typical starters and main course dishes. Try to elicit some vocabulary from the menu on page 20. Tell students to read the menu and check comprehension. Ask if anyone can explain what *vegetarian* means (not containing meat or fish). Ask students to name the vegetarian dishes on the menu.

Answers

Mushrooms in garlic, Asparagus with Hollandaise sauce, Goat's cheese salad, Grilled aubergines with parmesan, Red pepper and mushroom tart

■ Listening *Taking an order*

1 Ask students to read sentences 1–6. Check comprehension. Play the recording and then ask students to compare their answers in pairs. Play the recording again, pausing so students can check and correct their answers. Check answers around the class.

Answers

| 1 true | 2 false | 3 false | 4 true | 5 false | 6 false |

2 Tell students to look at the server's order pad and try to complete the order. Ask them to compare their answers in pairs. Play the recording again and let them check their answers. Check answers orally around the class.

Answers

1 salmon with dill sauce, 1 goat's cheese salad

Ask students to turn to the Listening script on page 68 and practise reading in groups of three, swapping roles. Go around and monitor their performance, helping where necessary. If the students have difficulty with their pronunciation or intonation, make a note of problem areas and model these again afterwards, with students repeating after you. Suggest one or two groups perform their dialogues in front of the class.

■ Language study

Expressions to learn

Ask students to read the expressions aloud, and check their pronunciation and intonation. Ask them to learn the expressions for homework.

New words to use

Ask students to read the words aloud and check pronunciation. Tell them to check any unfamiliar words in the Wordlist. Ask the class to learn the new words for homework.

Structures to practise

a/an, the

Point out that *an* is used before words beginning with the vowels: *a, e, i, o, u*. This is to make them easier to say. Draw students' attention to the explanation in their books, and ask them to study the example sentences. Give more examples of the rule if necessary:

*We're using **an** English book. **The** book is called Highly Recommended.*
*She's eating **a** sandwich. **The** sandwich is ham and cheese.*

Another way of contrasting the use of *a* and *the* is by explaining it as the general contrasted with the specific:

*Can we have **a** table? **The** table by the window is reserved.*
*Would you like **a** bottle of wine? We'd like **the** Chablis.*

3 Tell students to write the exercise and compare their answers in pairs. Go over the answers with the whole class.

    Answers

    | 1 an | 2 the | 3 a | 4 an, the | 5 a | 6 a, the |

    a/an, some
    Read through the example sentences and explain the difference between countable and uncountable nouns. Give more examples in two columns on the board: *a restaurant, a pen, a menu; some sugar, some toast, some information*. Give more examples orally and get students to say *a/an* or *some* depending on whether the noun is countable or uncountable. Add these to the lists on the board. Point out we usually use *a/an* instead of one: ***A** glass of water, please. / There's **a** guest at reception. / Do you have **a** parking space?* You could also explain that uncountable nouns can usually be made countable by putting a suitable phrase in front of them, such as: *a glass of (wine), a cup of (coffee), a slice of (bread)*, etc.

4 Ask students to read sentences 1–8 and then fill the gaps. Let them compare their answers in pairs. Go over the answers with the whole class.

    Answers

    | 1 some | 3 some | 5 some | 7 a |
    | 2 A | 4 an | 6 a | 8 some |

- **Listening** *Are you ready to order?*

    Ask students to name the different meals of the day: *breakfast, lunch, dinner*. Elicit some examples of typical food for these meals. Draw three columns on the board for the three meals and write the food in as students suggest it. You may want to point out the difference between an *English breakfast* (a large breakfast, usually of cereal, egg and bacon, toast, and tea or coffee); and a *continental breakfast* (a light breakfast, usually of coffee, and bread or croissant with butter or jam).

5 Tell students they are going to hear three different dialogues between waiting staff and guests. Ask students if they can predict the words to complete the expressions in sentences 1–6. Ask students to check their answers as they listen, and play the recording. Go over the answers with the whole class.

    Answers

    | 1 bacon | 3 soup | 5 sandwich |
    | 2 tea | 4 mushroom | 6 salad |

6 If students have not already copied the three columns written on the board prior to exercise 5, tell them to do so. Ask them to complete the columns as they listen, and play the recording again. Let them check their answers in pairs, and then check the answers around the class column by column. If necessary, model and practise any difficult phrases, asking students to repeat after you.

    Answers

    breakfast: coffee, croissant, egg and bacon, pot of tea, toast
    lunch: mushroom soup, cheese and ham toasted sandwich, chef's salad, bread
    dinner: basil and tomato soup, mushroom risotto, glass of dry white wine, water

    Ask students to turn to the Listening script on page 68. Students practise the dialogues in pairs, swapping roles. Go around and monitor their performance helping where necessary. When students have practised enough, ask them to improvise the dialogues from memory, using their menus from exercise 6.

- **Activity**

    Tell students they are going to create a simple menu and then practise taking orders. If necessary, revise important words and information needed. Divide the class into pairs and draw their attention to the menu on page 20 to use as a model. Go around the class, helping where necessary. When students have created the menu, ask them to practise making and taking orders. Again, go around helping where necessary. Go over general problems with the class, particularly any expressions you heard that were impolite or inappropriate.

    More words to use

    Ask students to read the words aloud, and check pronunciation and comprehension. Ask them to learn the phrases for homework.

10 Desserts and cheese

- **Situations/functions**
  Presenting a dessert menu
  Recommending dishes
- **Structures**
  some, any
- **Desserts and cheese**

Revision of Unit 9

Expressions to learn
Give students prompts to elicit the typical phrases that waiting staff use, from the arrival of customers to ordering the meal: *your table / coats? / menu and wine list / aperitif? / order? / wine?*

New words to use
Recycle as suggested in Unit 2, using flashcards.

More words to use
Ask students to brainstorm the names of different meats, cuts of beef, and some fish.

Other revision suggestions
- Ask the names of the different meals and elicit examples of typical menus.
- Revise *a/an, some* with countable and uncountable nouns, using flashcards.
- Revise *a/an, the* by asking students to fill in the gaps in the following sentences:
  1 She would like .... sandwich for lunch.
  2 .... sandwich is ham and cheese.
  3 I'd like .... orange juice.
  4 .... orange juice doesn't have any ice.
  5 Mary is .... chef.
  6 .... chef is excellent.
- Get students to practise reading the first Listening script from Unit 9 in groups of three.
- Tell students to do the Activity from Unit 9, working with a different partner.

Starter
Read through the items on the dessert menu and specials board, asking students to repeat after you. Students can check any unfamiliar words in the Wordlist. If necessary, explain the difference between *cream* and *ice cream*. Ask students to look at the photographs and find them on the menu and specials board.

Answers
Lemon tart, Ice cream, French apple tart, Chocolate mousse

■ Listening *What's for dessert?*

1 Tell students they are going to hear two customers ordering desserts. Ask students to listen for the two dessert orders, and play the recording. If necessary, play the recording again and pause after each order is given. Let students compare their answers in pairs. Check their answers around the class.

Answers
| Woman: blackcurrant sorbet | Man: French apple tart and ice cream |

Ask students to turn to the Listening script on pages 68–9 and practise chorally. Model any difficult phrases and ask students to repeat after you. Ask students to practise the dialogue in groups of three, swapping roles. Go around and monitor their performance, helping and correcting where necessary.

2 Ask students to read the Expressions to learn, and check their pronunciation and intonation. Check comprehension. Read the examples in exercise 2. Ask students to improvise similar dialogues with a partner, choosing desserts from the menu and specials board.

■ Language study

Expressions to learn
Ask students to learn the expressions for homework.

New words to use
Ask students to read the list of words aloud and check their pronunciation. Tell them to check any unfamiliar words in the Wordlist. Ask students to learn the new words for homework.

Structures to practise
some, any

Read through the examples and explain the rules for using *some* and *any*. Give more examples of the use of *some* with polite offers and requests, and of *any* in questions. The distinction can be confusing for students as offers and requests are usually questions too.

3 Ask students to complete sentences 1–6, then compare answers in pairs. Go over the answers with the whole class.

Answers

| 1 any | 2 some | 3 some | 4 any | 5 some | 6 any |

4 Ask students to read the examples. Tell them to work in pairs to write three-line dialogues as in the example, using the information given in sentences 1–5. Remind students that they can use *sir* or *madam* in their responses: *Would you like it with cream or ice cream, madam?* Go around the class checking and correcting, particularly the use of *them* to refer to *profiteroles* in number 4.

Model answers

1 Could I have a coffee, please? / Would you like it with milk or without? / With milk, please.
2 I'd like some cheesecake, please. / Would you like it with cream or ice cream? / Ice cream, please.
3 Can I have the steak? / Would you like it with French fries or salad, sir? / French fries, please.
4 Could I have the profiteroles, please? / Would you like them with chocolate sauce or without, madam? / With chocolate sauce, please.
5 Can I have a salad, please? / Would you like it with French dressing or mayonnaise? / French dressing, please.

Ask the students to practise their dialogues in pairs, swapping roles. Go around and monitor pronunciation and intonation. Make a note of any problem areas and model these afterwards, with students repeating after you.

■ Listening *What about some cheese?*

Ask students to brainstorm as many types of cheese as they can. Ask them to describe some of the qualities of the cheeses (*hard, soft, blue*). If you live in a country where cheese is not often eaten, ask students to look at the photographs of the cheeses and describe what they can see. (There is one hard, one soft, and one blue.)

5 Ask students to look at the table of cheeses and the map of European countries. Read the names of the cheeses and ask students to repeat after you. Do the same with the names of the countries. Ask students to predict the answer by completing the table before listening. Play the recording, and let them check and correct their answers.

Answers

Mozzarella, soft, Italy
Manchego, hard, Spain
Gouda, hard, the Netherlands
Gruyère, hard, Switzerland
Camembert, soft, France
Stilton, blue, Britain
Danish Blue, blue, Denmark

6 Ask students to read the examples chorally. Tell them to work in pairs, asking about and describing the list of cheeses 1–6, following the examples.

Answers

1 Camembert is a soft cheese from France.
2 Stilton is a blue cheese from Britain.
3 Manchego is a hard cheese from Spain.
4 Danish Blue is a blue cheese from Denmark.
5 Mozzarella is a soft cheese from Italy.
6 Gouda is a hard cheese from the Netherlands.

Check answers around the class. Ask students to continue practising questions and answers, swapping roles. Go around checking and monitoring pronunciation and intonation, helping where necessary.

■ Activity

Tell students they are going to practise talking about desserts and cheese. If necessary, revise important words and information needed. Divide the class into pairs, Student A and Student B. Direct them to the correct page for each role, reminding them not to look at the other student's information. Draw their attention to the example dialogues to help give them an idea of what they are expected to do. When they have read the information, ask Student A (as the customer) to start by asking: *Excuse me, what kind of cheese is Emmenthal? What's it like?* Remind students the roles are then reversed, and Student A plays the part of the waiter. Go around the class, helping students where necessary. When they have finished, go over general problems with the class, particularly any expressions you heard that were impolite or inappropriate.

More words to use

Read the desserts and cheeses and ask students to repeat after you. Check pronunciation and comprehension. Use a map of the world to teach the countries and nationalities. Ask students to learn the words for homework.

11 Talking about wine

- **Situations/functions**
  Comparing wines
  Talking about countries and nationalities
- **Structures**
  Comparisons:
  -er than, *more ... than*, *not as ... as*
- **Names of wines, directions**

■ Revision of Unit 10

Expressions to learn

Write the gapfill expressions on the board and ask students to complete them:
I'm glad you .... it.
.... you .... the dessert menu?
I .... the French apple tart.
.... you .... it with cream or ice cream?

New words to use

Recycle as suggested in Unit 2, using flashcards.

More words to use

Ask students to brainstorm the names of different desserts and cheeses. Revise countries and nationalities using a map of the world.

Other revision suggestions

- Elicit the rules for *some* and *any*:
  In positive statements, and polite requests and offers we use ...? (*some*)
  In questions and negative statements we use ...? (*any*)
- Get students to practise the first Listening script from Unit 10 in groups of three.
- Tell students to do the Activity from Unit 10, working with a different partner.

■ Starter

Ask students to look at the picture of the wine labels and read the types of wines. List them on the board. For pronunciation practice, read the list aloud and ask students to repeat after you. Ask if they can add to the list of famous world wines.

Answers

Chardonnay, Chablis, Shiraz, Merlot (Chilean), Sauvignon Blanc, Rioja, Riesling, Zinfandel, Merlot (French), Cabernet Sauvignon, Pinot Grigio

■ Listening *Would you like to order some wine?*

1 Tell students they are going to hear two customers ordering wine with their meal. Ask them which three wines the customers choose to drink with their meal. Play the recording, then let students check their answers in pairs.

Answers

Sauvignon Blanc, Chardonnay, French Merlot

2 Elicit some of the qualities of wine: *red, white, dry, sweet, light, smooth, full-bodied*. Ask students to read sentences 1–6. Ask students to mark whether the statements are *true* or *false* as they listen, and play the recording again. Check the answers with the whole class.

Answers

| 1 false | 2 true | 3 true | 4 true | 5 false | 6 true |

Ask students to turn to the Listening script and practise reading in groups of three, swapping roles. Go around and monitor their performance, helping where necessary. If the students have difficulty with their pronunciation or intonation, make a note of any problem areas and model these again afterwards, with students repeating after you.

Suggest one or two groups perform the dialogue in front of the class.

■ Language study

Expressions to learn

Ask students to read the expressions aloud, and check their pronunciation and intonation. Ask them to learn the expressions for homework.

New words to use

Ask the class to read the words aloud, and check pronunciation. Review the points of the compass: *north, south, east*, and *west*. Tell them to check any unfamiliar words in the Wordlist. Ask students to learn the new words for homework.

Structures to practise

Comparisons

Read the first example. Write *sweeter than* on the board. Explain that all one- and two-syllable adjectives form their comparative in this way: add *-er + than*. Brainstorm a list of these adjectives and write them on the board with their comparative form: *fresh–fresher, smooth–smoother*, etc. Point out the spelling change in short adjectives ending in the letter y: *dry–drier, busy–busier*.

Read the second example. Write *more expensive than* on the board. Explain that longer adjectives form their comparatives in this way: *more* + adjective + *than*. Ask students if they know any more 3-syllable (or longer) adjectives: *beautiful, full-bodied, expensive*, etc. Tell students two important exceptions to these rules are the adjectives *good* and *bad*, which have the comparative forms *better* and *worse*.

Read the third example. Write *not as dry as* on the board. Explain that this is a negative comparison formed with *not as* + adjective + *as*. Give more examples: *Paris isn't as big as Mexico City. The café isn't as expensive as the restaurant.* Ask students for more examples.

3 Tell students to write the exercise and compare answers in pairs. Go over the answers with the whole class.

Answers

1 busier	3 more expensive	5 cheaper
2 closer	4 better	6 not as smooth

■ Listening *Wines around the world*

There are a lot of new wine names in this Listening, so spend some time pre-teaching. Try to brainstorm some of the wines from France, Italy, Spain, and the New World that are mentioned in the recording. Write the names on the board and practise pronunciation, asking students to repeat after you.

4 Tell students they are going to hear a talk given by a wine expert. Ask students to match the wines with a country or region as they listen, and play the recording. Let them check their answers in pairs. Go over the answers with the whole class.

Answers

| 1 d | 2 g | 3 a | 4 b | 5 f | 6 e | 7 c |

5 Test students on the points of the compass, and then elicit the points in between: *north-east, south-west*, etc. Read the example sentences, paying particular attention to the prepositions and definite article. Ask students to underline the correct alternative in sentences 1–5. Play the recording. Let them check their answers in pairs and, if necessary, play the recording again. Check the answers with the whole class.

Answers

| 1 east | 2 south-west | 3 north | 4 north | 5 south |

6 Draw students' attention to the list of wines and countries. Tell them to look at the text with the missing words 1–7, and ask them to predict the country or wine to make a summary of the information in exercise 5. If necessary, play the recording again. Let students compare answers in pairs. Go over answers with the whole class. Ask one or two students to read their summaries to the class.

Answers

1 Champagne	3 Bordeaux	5 Frascati	7 Spain
2 France	4 Italian	6 Port	

■ Activity

Tell students they are going to practise talking about wine. If necessary, revise important words and information needed. Divide the class into pairs, Student A and Student B. Draw their attention to the example dialogue and direct them to the webpage on page 65. There is quite a lot of information, so students need to be given plenty of time. When they have read the information, ask Student A to start by asking about one of the red wines. Encourage Student B to compare wines in their reply, as in the example dialogue. It may be easier for Student B to talk about the red wines and Student A to talk about the white wines. Go around the class, helping students where necessary. When they have finished, go over general problems with the class, particularly any difficulties giving comparisons.

More words to use

Ask students to repeat the words after you and check pronunciation and comprehension. Ask them to learn the lists for homework.

12 Dealing with requests

- **Situations/functions**
  Helping guests in hotels and restaurants
- **Structures**
  I'll get you some/one/another/some more
- **Customer care advice**

■ Revision of Unit 11

Expressions to learn

Write the gapfill expressions on the board and ask students to complete them:

*The Sauvignon Blanc is drier .... the Riesling.
It isn't .... dry .... the Pinot Grigio.
The French Merlot is .... expensive .... the Chilean.*

New words to use / More words to use

Elicit words related to wine by asking questions: *How do you open a bottle of wine? How do you know the name of a wine?*, etc. Practise direction words using a map. Give one central city, e.g. Madrid. Ask questions for students to relate directions to the given city or the country as a whole: Q *Where's Seville?* / A *It's in the south of Spain* or *It's south of Madrid.*

Other revision suggestions

- Get students to practise making comparisons on topics other than wine: food, hotels, cities, etc.
- Tell students to do the Activity from Unit 11, working with a different partner.

■ Starter

Ask students to look at the pictures and guess what the requests are.

Answers

| a | He wants a taxi. | c | He wants laundry service. |
| b | She wants some more bread. | d | She wants another (clean) glass. |

Ask students for more examples of requests that guests make in hotels and restaurants. Check if any of your students have worked in the hotel and catering industry and, if so, ask them about their experiences of dealing with such requests.

■ Listening *I'll get you some now*

1 Tell students they are going to hear seven dialogues in which guests make requests. Tell them to look at the exercise and check any unfamiliar words in the Wordlist. Ask if they can predict the missing words in any of the requests. Play the recording, and ask students to check and correct their predictions. Let them compare their answers in pairs. Go over the answers with the whole class.

Answers

| 1 Can | 3 Could | 5 like | 7 glass |
| 2 like | 4 laundry service | 6 What time | |

2 Read through responses a–g, asking students to repeat after you. Explain the importance of the correct intonation, as responses to guests should always sound polite. Tell students to work in pairs, matching each response with a request in exercise 1. Play the recording again, and let students check and correct their answers. If necessary, go over answers with the whole class.

Answers

| a 5 | b 3 | c 1 | d 2 | e 7 | f 4 | g 6 |

Ask students to take it in turns to practise the requests and responses. Go around and monitor their performance, helping where necessary. Listen in particular for polite intonation. Make a note of any problem areas and model these again afterwards, with students repeating after you. When students have practised enough, ask them to close their books and improvise the exchanges from memory. You could give them some prompts to help them: *a taxi, a glass of wine, some more bread*, etc.

■ Language study

Expressions to learn

Ask students to read the expressions aloud, and check pronunciation and intonation. Ask them to learn the expressions for homework.

New words to use

Ask students to read the words aloud and check pronunciation. Tell them to check any unfamiliar words in the Wordlist, and learn the new words for homework.

Structures to practise

Offering help

Write on the board: .... *map*, ... *bread*, ... *spoon*. Ask students if the nouns are countable or uncountable, and write *some* or *a* in the gaps.

Draw students' attention to the example sentences in the book. Ask them to read the first and second examples. Explain that we use *one* to refer back to a countable noun (first example), and *some* to refer back to an uncountable noun (second example).

Read the following sentences and get students to give replies using *I'll get...*, both chorally and individually: *I'd like a coffee. / I'd like some cheese. / I'd like a beer. / I'd like a glass of wine. / I'd like some milk. / I'd like some ice.* Ask them to read the third and fourth examples. Explain that *one + one = another* (countable nouns), and *some + some = some more* (uncountable nouns). Read the following sentences and get students to give replies using *I'll get...*, both chorally and individually: *This glass is dirty. / This coffee's cold. / There isn't any more mayonnaise. / This beer's flat. / There isn't any bread left. / This bottle is corked.*

3 Ask students to read sentences 1–8 and check comprehension. Tell students to write the exercise, then compare answers in pairs. Go over the answers with the whole class.

Answers

1 I'll get you one.	5 I'll get you one.
2 I'll get you some more.	6 I'll get you another.
3 I'll bring you another.	7 I'll bring you another.
4 I'll get you some.	8 I'll bring you some more.

Ask students to practise the requests and responses in pairs, swapping roles. Remind them to pay attention to polite intonation for the responses. They can also apologize before giving the response.

■ Listening *Customer care*

Elicit from students some basic examples of good customer care: *smile, be polite*, etc. Ask students if they can give you examples of hotel guests with special needs: *elderly guests, disabled people*, etc.

4 Tell students they are going to hear a dialogue between a reception trainee and the trainer. Read situations 1–4 and check comprehension. Tell students to listen for the customer care advice in the different situations, and play the recording. If necessary, pause after each piece of advice on the four situations. Check answers around the class.

Answers

1 Welcome with a warm smile; be polite and friendly at all times; don't keep people waiting long.
2 Answer the call within three rings; apologize for any delay; use the customer's name in conversation.
3 Find out what they would like; be patient and helpful.
4 Smile at customers who are waiting; don't keep them waiting long.

5 Ask students to work in pairs to write a dialogue between a hotel receptionist and a woman business traveller, using the notes given. Remind students to keep the customer care advice in mind. Get them to practise speaking their dialogues in pairs, swapping roles.

Model answer

Woman:	I'd like to book a wake-up call.
Reception:	Certainly. What time would you like it?
Woman:	At 07.00, please. And my suit needs dry cleaning.
Reception:	I'll send someone up for it right away.
Woman:	Thank you. Can I book a taxi for this evening?
Reception:	Of course. What time would you like it?
Woman:	7.45, please. Is there Internet access in my room?
Reception:	One moment, I'll check for you. Yes, there is.
Woman:	Good. And is the sauna open now?
Reception:	It's open until midnight.

■ Activity

Tell students they are going to practise dealing with requests. If necessary, revise important words and information needed. Divide the class into pairs, Student A and Student B. Direct them to the correct page for each role, reminding them not to look at the other student's information. When they have read the information, ask Student A to start by saying: *Excuse me, my room is very noisy. Could I move to a quieter one?* Remind Student B they need to choose the best answer for the request – the answers are not in the correct order. Go around the class, helping students where necessary. When the ten requests and answers have been made, go over general problems with the class, particularly any expressions you heard that were impolite or inappropriate.

More words to use

Ask students to read the words aloud, and check pronunciation. Remind students that *some*, not *a* or a number, is used before uncountable nouns. Ask students to learn the list of uncountable nouns for homework.

13 Describing dishes

Situations/functions
Explaining dishes to customers
Setting a table

Structures
Present Simple Passive

Main course dishes, cutlery

■ Revision of Unit 12

Expressions to learn
Say the customer prompts below, or write them on the board. Tell students to respond as hotel or restaurant staff: *We'd like a table on the terrace. / Can we have some water? / This spoon is dirty. / We've finished our wine. / What time does the Exchange Bureau open?* If necessary, continue with variations on these prompts.

New words to use
Recycle as suggested in Unit 2, using flashcards.

More words to use
Ask students to name as many uncountable nouns as they can. Encourage them to use *some* before the nouns: *some bread, some advice*, etc.

Other revision suggestions
- Revise customer care phrases by giving prompts: *welcome guests, answer phone, special needs customers*, etc.
- Tell students to do the Activity from Unit 12, working with a different partner.

■ Starter
Ask students to read aloud the list of dishes from the menu. Check pronunciation. If necessary, model pronunciation with students repeating after you. Help students with any new words by referring to the photographs (there is one of each item on the menu), or give them time to check in the Wordlist. Revise the meaning of *vegetarian*. Ask students to find two meat dishes, three fish dishes, and four vegetarian dishes on the menu. Encourage them to give their answers orally.

Answers
> Two meat dishes: Pork chops with port wine and plum sauce, Lamb cutlets with rosemary and garlic
> Three fish dishes: Smoked salmon blinis, Salmon coulibiac, Mixed seafood for two
> Four vegetarian dishes: Asparagus with Hollandaise sauce, Mushroom and red wine pâté, Penne arrabbiata, Grilled aubergine with red peppers

■ Listening *What's it made from?*
Pre-teach potentially difficult vocabulary: *chilli, tomato, garlic, basil, pine nuts, rice, onions, hard boiled eggs, puff pastry, lobster, scallops, mussels*. Model the pronunciation and get students to repeat after you so they will recognize them when they hear them.

1 Ask students to tick three dishes on the menu that they hear, and play the recording.

Answers
> Penne arrabiata, Salmon coulibiac, Mixed seafood

2 Read through sentences 1–6 and ask students to predict the missing words. Play the recording again, and ask them to check and correct their answers. Go over the answers with the whole class. Model the sentences and ask students to repeat after you chorally and individually.

Answers
> 1 pasta   3 made   5 contains
> 2 consists 4 baked   6 served

Ask students to work in pairs and take it in turns to describe the dishes. Go around and monitor their performance, helping where necessary. If the students have difficulty with their pronunciation or intonation, make a note of any problem areas and model these again afterwards, asking students to repeat after you.

■ Language study

Expressions to learn
Ask students to read the expressions aloud, and check pronunciation and intonation. Ask them to learn the expressions for homework.

Unit 13 Describing dishes

New words to use

Ask students to read the words aloud and check pronunciation. Tell them to check any unfamiliar words in the Wordlist. Ask the class to learn the new words for homework.

Structures to practise

Present Simple Passive

Elicit the Present Simple of the verb *be* in all persons and write it on the board. Write other regular and irregular verbs on the board and elicit or give the past participle: *make–made, close–closed, eat–eaten, play–played*, etc. Explain that the passive is formed with the verb *be* and the past participle of the verb. Elicit examples using the verbs above: *Champagne .... in France.* / *The restaurant .... on Mondays.* / *Pasta dishes .... in Italy.* / *Football .... all over the world.* Draw students' attention to the first example in the book, showing how the sentence is made passive. Ask them to identify the subject and the object of the first example. Point out how the object of the sentence (*ice cream*), becomes the subject of the passive sentence. Do the same with the second example.

3 Read through sentences 1–6, asking students to identify the object of each sentence, and then make the sentence passive. You may have to direct students to the list of Irregular verbs on page 111 so they can check irregular past participles. Get students to write the exercise and compare answers in pairs. Go over the answers again with the whole class.

Answers

1. Pasta is made from flour, eggs, and salt.
2. A Margarita is made with tequila.
3. Guests are told about the hotel facilities.
4. Dinner is served from 7.30 to 11.00.
5. Dressing is made from oil and vinegar.
6. Your order is taken at the table.

■ Listening *Do you know how to lay a table?*

Ask students to work in pairs to predict the names of the items in the picture of the place setting.

4 Play the recording, and let students check their answers in pairs. If necessary, tell them to refer to the Listening script to check their answers. Go over the answers with the whole class. (The word *cover* used in the script is an alternative to *place setting*.)

Answers

| 1 g | 3 f | 5 i | 7 h | 9 c | 11 a |
| 2 e | 4 j | 6 k | 8 l | 10 b | 12 d |

5 Ask students to make sentences using the correct passive form. Remind them that knife and fork, salt and pepper, and dessert fork and spoon need *are*, not *is*. After checking their answers, tell them to practise the instructions with a partner.

Answers

The tablecloth is placed on the table.
The napkin is folded and placed on the table.
The knife and fork are placed each side of the plate.
The wine glass is put above the soup spoon.
The salt and pepper are put in the middle of the table.
The main course plate is taken away when the main course is finished.
The dessert spoon and fork are brought with the dessert menu.
A flower arrangement is placed next to the salt and pepper.

■ Activity

Tell students they are going to practise describing dishes. If necessary, revise important words and information needed. Divide the class into pairs, Student A and Student B. Direct them to the correct page for each role, reminding them not to look at the other student's information. When they have read the information, ask Student A to start by asking Student B about their three dishes. Go around the class, helping students where necessary. Encourage them to note down the important information. When the roles have been reversed, tell students to compare the tables they completed. Go over general problems with the class, particularly any difficulties using the prepositions in the expressions: consist **of**, made **from**, served **with**.

More words to use

Read through the cooking methods and make sure students understand the difference between them. Ask students to read the words aloud, and check their pronunciation. Read the names of the five sauces and ask students to research the ingredients of each sauce for homework. Also, ask them to learn both lists for homework.

Unit 13 Describing dishes

14 Dealing with complaints

- **Situations/functions**
  Apologizing to guests/customers
  Talking about the past
- **Structures**
  Past Simple
- **Negative adjectives**
  dirty, *noisy*, etc.

■ Revision of Unit 13

Expressions to learn
Ask students questions about dishes from Unit 13 to elicit responses beginning: *It consists of…, It's made from…, It contains…, It's served with… .*

New words to use
Recycle as suggested in Unit 2, using flashcards.

More words to use
Ask students to brainstorm all the cooking methods they know. Check their homework from Unit 13 by asking about the five sauces:

Aioli – egg yolks, lemon juice, garlic, olive oil, salt and pepper; *Bearnaise* – egg yolks, butter, dry white wine, vinegar, tarragon, shallots, salt and pepper; *Béchamel* – hot milk, butter, flour, grated nutmeg, salt and pepper; *Hollandaise* – egg yolks, lemon juice, butter, salt and pepper; *Mornay* – as Béchamel plus grated cheese.

Other revision suggestions
- Get students to describe a place setting using passive forms.
- Tell students to do the Activity from Unit 13, working with a different partner.

■ Starter

Ask students what kind of problem situations guests often complain about and how staff could reply. Tell students to look at the pictures and identify the five problem situations. You may want to wait until after exercise 1 to confirm their answers.

Answers

a The car park is full.
b They're unhappy about their rooms.
c He didn't receive his message.
d They haven't been served yet.
e His steak is overcooked.

■ Listening *What is there to complain about?*

1 Tell students they are going to listen to the complaints of five hotel guests and restaurant customers, and the staff's responses. Read key words 1–5 and the problems a–e, and ask students to repeat after you. Check comprehension. Ask students to match the key words and phrases to the problems as they listen, and play the recording. Let students compare their answers in pairs. Play the recording again, pausing after each dialogue if necessary, and go over the answers with the whole class.

Answers

1 b   2 d   3 e   4 a   5 c

2 Ask students to read the two lists of sentences and to work in pairs to match 1–5 with a–e. Let students check their answers as they listen, and play the recording. Go over the answers with the whole class.

Answers

1 c   2 a   3 b   4 e   5 d

Ask students to turn to the Listening script on page 70. Divide the class into two groups: guests/customers, and reception/waiter/waitress. Ask them to read the dialogues aloud chorally. Note any problem areas and model these with students repeating after you. Tell them to swap roles. Ask students to continue practising in pairs. Go around and monitor their performance, helping where necessary. Suggest students perform the dialogues in front of the class.

■ Language study

Expressions to learn
Ask students to read the expressions aloud, and check their pronunciation and intonation. Ask them to learn the expressions for homework.

New words to use
Read the list of words with students repeating after you. Check their pronunciation. Tell them to check any unfamiliar words in the Wordlist. Ask students to learn the new words for homework.

Structures to practise

Past Simple (Regular verbs)

Write the two example sentences on the board. Explain that these are finished actions in the past. Elicit or give rules for the formation of the Past Simple: regular verbs add *-ed* (to a verb ending in a consonant), or *-d* (to a verb ending in the letter *-e*).

3 Draw students' attention to the example. Ask students to make sentences from the prompts given in sentences 1–6 in the same way, with the verb in the Past Simple. Tell students to write the exercise and compare answers in pairs. Go over the answers with the whole class. As students read their answers, check pronunciation of the Past Simple verb endings.

Answers

1 They arrived at the hotel yesterday.
2 She asked for dessert without cream.
3 The chef cooked a wonderful meal.
4 The guests enjoyed their stay.
5 He keyed in the reservations data.
6 The waiter opened a bottle of champagne.

Past Simple (Irregular verbs)

Write the two example sentences on the board and point out the irregularity. Refer students to the Irregular Verbs on page 111 to confirm the Past Simple of these verbs.

4 Ask students to read sentences 1–6. Check comprehension. Tell students to use the list of Irregular verbs and complete the sentences in the Past Simple. Let students compare their answers in pairs. Go over the answers with the whole class.

Answers

1 told
2 went
3 spoke
4 met
5 wrote
6 ate, paid

■ Listening *I'll look into it for you*

Before playing the recording, elicit what action students would take in the following situations: a customer says their beer is flat; a guest says their room isn't ready; a guest complains about the noise from the room next door; a customer complains that their food is undercooked; a restaurant customer says the table is too small; a customer complains about a dirty napkin. Write any unfamiliar vocabulary on the board and give students time to check it in the Wordlist.

5 Tell students they are going to hear six short complaints and responses. Tell them to note down the problem in the first column in the table, and the staff action taken in the second. Draw their attention to the example. Ask students to complete the table as they listen, and play the recording. Let them compare their answers in pairs. Play the recording again, pausing after each dialogue if necessary, and go over the answers with the whole class.

Answers

2 room isn't ready	send up someone from housekeeping
3 noise from room next door	look into it
4 fish undercooked	talk to the chef, bring another
5 table too small	change table
6 dirty fork	get a clean one

6 Ask students to work in pairs to write dialogues from their notes. Go around the class, helping where necessary. Get students to practise their dialogues in pairs, swapping roles. Go around the class and monitor polite intonation for staff responses. Suggest students perform the dialogues in front of the class.

■ Activity

Tell students they are going to practise dealing with complaints. If necessary, revise important words and information needed. Divide the class into pairs, Student A and Student B. Direct them to the correct page for each role, reminding them not to look at the other student's information. When they have read the information, ask Student A to start by complaining: *Excuse me, the TV in my room is broken.* Go around the class, helping students where necessary. Encourage them to note down the solutions offered by Student B. Remind students the roles are then reversed, and Student B makes complaints and notes down the solutions offered. When they have finished, tell students to check the accuracy of the information they noted down. Go over general problems with the class, particularly examples of forgetting to apologize or expressions you heard that were impolite or inappropriate.

More words to use

Read the list of negative adjectives often used in customer complaints. Ask students to repeat after you. Tell students to check any unfamiliar words in the Wordlist and learn them for homework.

Jobs and workplaces

◈ **Situations/functions**
Showing people around
Talking about jobs

◈ **Structures**
this/that, these/those
here/there
responsible to, responsible for

◈ **Jobs, workplaces, and work routines**

■ Revision of Unit 14

Expressions to learn
Ask students to think of as many guest and customer complaints as they can. Ask how staff should respond in each case.

New words to use / More words to use
Brainstorm all the negative adjectives used in customer complaints from Unit 14. Help with mime, prompts, and by giving opposites. Recycle other words as suggested in Unit 2, using flashcards.

Other revision suggestions
- Re-elicit the rules for forming the Past Simple of regular verbs.
- Test knowledge of the Past Simple of irregular verbs from Unit 14: *leave, have, tell, go, speak, meet, write, eat, pay*.
- Tell students to do the Activity from Unit 14, working with a different partner.

■ Starter

Ask students to name the work areas in the photographs (reception/front office, and kitchen). Elicit the job titles of the people who are working on reception/front office: *receptionist, cashier*. Elicit the job title of the people working in the kitchen: *chefs*. Ask students if they know the titles of the different chefs: *head chef, sous chef* /suː ʃef/, *chef de partie* /ʃef də ˈpɑːti/, *pastry chef, commis chef* /ˈkɒmi ʃef/. (Their different duties will be covered in exercise 5.)

■ Listening *Let's start at front office*

Check if any students are working, or have worked, in front office. If so, ask which IT software systems are used for taking reservations, processing reservations, check in and check out, and contacts with travel agencies. (*Fidelio* is the system for processing guest reservations, check in, check out and payment. *Galileo* is the name of the central reservations system. *Sabre* provides the link with travel agencies. These are used worldwide in most hotels.)

1 Tell students they are going to hear a personnel officer showing someone around front office. Ask students to read sentences 1–6. Check comprehension. Ask students to mark the sentences *true* or *false* as they listen, and play the recording. Tell them to check their answers in pairs. Play the recording again, pausing after each section if necessary. Go over the answers with the whole class.

Answers
| 1 false | 2 true | 3 false | 4 true | 5 true | 6 false |

2 Ask students to read sentences 1–6, and try to predict the missing words. Play the recording again and let them check their answers. Go over the answers with the whole class.

Answers
| 1 Here's | 3 receptionist | 5 These, those |
| 2 This | 4 That's | 6 systems |

■ Language study

Expressions to learn
Ask students to read the expressions aloud, and check their pronunciation and intonation. Ask them to learn the expressions for homework.

New words to use
Read the words aloud with students repeating after you. Tell them to check any unfamiliar words in the Wordlist. Ask students to learn the new words for homework.

Structures to practise

this/that, these/those, here/there

Ask students to look at the pictures. Relate the example sentences to the pictures. Explain *this* (singular), *these* (plural), and *here* refer to places, objects, or people near the speaker; *that* (singular), *those* (plural), and *there* refer to places, objects, or people at a distance from the speaker. Demonstrate with examples around the class using students, books, pens, door, windows, etc.

3 Draw students' attention to the examples, and tell them to practise the forms with a partner by using objects around the room.

responsible to, responsible for

Ask students to read the examples. Elicit the rules: you are *responsible to* a person (they are your boss); you are *responsible for* doing something (it's your job). Explain to students you can also be responsible for a person (in charge of them): *The head receptionist is **responsible for** the porters.* Similarly, explain you also can be *responsible for* something (in charge of it): *The chef is **responsible for** the kitchen.*

4 Ask students to complete the sentences and check their answers in pairs. Go over the answers with the whole class.

Answers

1 responsible to	3 responsible for	5 responsible to
2 responsible for	4 responsible for	6 responsible for

■ Listening ... *and in the kitchen*

5 Tell students they are going to hear a continuation of the tour in the first Listening. Read through the kitchen staff titles and duties with students. Check pronunciation and comprehension. Ask students to work in pairs and predict which kitchen staff do which duties. Play the recording and let students check their answers as they listen. Go over the answers with the whole class.

Answers

1 d 2 f 3 b 4 e 5 a 6 c

6 Ask students to read sentences 1–6, and try to predict the missing words in pairs. Play the recording again, pausing if necessary, and let students correct their answers as they listen. Go over the answers with the whole class.

Answers

1 main	3 handle, dishes	5 duties
2 prepares	4 bakes	6 sharpen, clean

At this point, you could refer students to the Listening script on page 70 for reading practice.

7 Draw students' attention to the example. This combines the duties listed in exercise 5 with some extra information from the second Listening. Tell students to work in pairs and explain the different jobs and duties of the kitchen staff. Go around the class, helping where necessary. Encourage students to make complete sentences.

■ Activity

Tell students they are going to practise describing job positions and responsibilities. If necessary, revise important words and information needed. Divide the class into pairs and draw their attention to the organization chart and example. When they have looked at the information, ask students to take turns describing job positions on it. (There are twelve different positions in total, which means students can describe six each.) Go around the class, helping students where necessary. Go over general problems with the class, particularly any mistakes using the prepositions in the expressions: *responsible **to*** and *responsible **for***.

More words to use

Ask students to repeat after you as you read through the different categories. Check pronunciation. Tell them to check any unfamiliar words in the Wordlist, and learn them for homework.

16 Explaining and instructing

Situations/functions
Explaining how to do things
Talking about food preparation

Structures
must, have to, don't have to, mustn't

Hygiene

■ Revision of Unit 15

Expressions to learn / New words to use

Ask students questions to elicit the job titles of front office staff and kitchen staff. Ask who they are responsible to. Ask who/what they are responsible for. Ask what work they handle and what duties they do.

More words to use

Brainstorm all the kitchen equipment and kitchenware terms. Recycle them, and the words in New words to use not yet revised, as suggested in Unit 2, using flashcards.

Other revision suggestions

- Ask students to tell you about the different computerized systems used in front office.
- Get students to give you example sentences around the class using: *this/that, these/those, here/there*.
- Tell students to do the Activity from Unit 15, working with a different partner.

■ Starter

Ask students what jobs the people in the photographs are doing. Read the list of words 1–9 and check pronunciation. Ask students to match them with the items in the pictures.

Answers

| 1 c | 2 d | 3 f | 4 g | 5 h | 6 a | 7 b | 8 e | 9 i |

■ Listening *How to do it right*

Check if any of your students have worked as a kitchen porter. If so, ask what duties they did. Elicit from all students the following vegetable preparation verbs: *wash, peel, julienne, cut/cut up, sort, slice, scrape, boil, chop, break, cook, strain*. Then elicit the names of the vegetables: *carrots, potatoes, onions, broccoli*. Check if any of your students have worked as a room attendant. If so, ask what duties they did. Elicit from all students the following vocabulary: *sheet, pillow case, towel, dirty linen, trolley, soap, shampoo, bath/shower gel, body lotion*. Then elicit the verbs: *strip, put, clean, change, replace*.

1 Tell students they are going to listen to two dialogues: the first between two chefs in the kitchen; and the second between two room attendants in a hotel bedroom. Read through questions 1–3 for Dialogue 1. Play the recording and pause at the end of the first dialogue. Ask students to discuss the questions in pairs. Play Dialogue 1 again, and ask them to check their answers. Repeat the procedure with questions 4–6 for Dialogue 2.

Answers

Dialogue 1
1 The lunch vegetables.
2 They must wash their hands.
3 No, they boil them with their skins on.

Dialogue 2
4 She has to strip the beds.
5 She cleans the bathroom.
6 soap, shampoo, bath/shower gel, body lotion

2 Tell students to read sentences 1–8 and try to fill in the gaps in pairs. Tell students to check and correct their answers as they listen, and play the recording. If necessary, play the recording again and let students check their answers. Go over the answers with the whole class.

Answers

| 1 have to | 3 Cut | 5 chop | 7 dirty |
| 2 must | 4 Do/have to | 6 mustn't | 8 must |

Divide the class into kitchen porters and room attendants. Get them to call out the different jobs that they have to do: *I have to peel the carrots. / I have to strip the beds*, etc. Give prompts to generate a range of vocabulary.

■ Language study

Expressions to learn

Ask students to read the expressions aloud, and check their pronunciation and intonation. Ask them to learn the expressions for homework.

New words to use

Ask students to read the words aloud and check pronunciation. Tell them to check any unfamiliar words in the Wordlist. Ask the class to learn the new words for homework.

Structures to practise

must, have to, don't have to, mustn't

Draw students' attention to the two example sentences for **obligation**. Explain *must* is used when the speaker thinks something is important; and *have to* when there is a rule of the job or situation. Elicit or give more examples: *You **must** be polite to guests at all times. / Guests **must** report to reception when they arrive. / He **has to** start work at 6 a.m. during the week. / Today, you **have to** help the chef with the sauces.*

Draw students' attention to the example sentence for **no obligation**. Explain *don't have to* is used when there **isn't** a rule of the job or situation. Elicit or give more examples: *He **doesn't have to** start work at 6 a.m. at the weekend. / You **don't have to** scrape the potatoes.*

Draw students' attention to the example sentence for **prohibition**. Explain *mustn't* is similar to giving a negative order: *You mustn't smoke in the kitchen = Don't smoke in the kitchen!* Elicit or give more examples: *You **mustn't** keep guests waiting. / You **mustn't** be rude to customers.*

3 Ask students to complete the exercise, and compare their answers in pairs. Go over the answers with the whole class.

Answers

1 must	3 don't have to	5 must	7 must
2 have to	4 have to	6 mustn't	

■ Listening *Kitchen hygiene*

Elicit from students some of the basics of kitchen hygiene. Prompt them if necessary to elicit: *wash hands* (using hand basin, not food preparation sinks), *clean work surfaces, sweep and wash floors, wash and dry utensils, deal with rubbish.*

4 Tell students they are going to hear a head chef talking to the staff about kitchen hygiene. Ask students to match the phrases, and play the recording. Get them to compare their answers in pairs. Play the recording again and let them check and correct their answers. Go over the answers with the whole class.

Answers

1 f	2 d	3 a	4 c	5 b	6 e

Ask students to rewrite the pairs of phrases as sentences to make a list of hygiene regulations. Point out that they need a subject for the sentences: **Kitchen staff / They** *must always wash their hands in the hand basin.* Get them to practise saying the regulations with a partner.

5 Tell students to read the customer care ideas. Check comprehension. Read the example sentence and ask students to do the same with the other ideas to make a list of customer care regulations using *must* and *mustn't*.

Model answers

You must be polite at all times.
You mustn't keep customers waiting long.
You must answer the phone quickly.
You must remember the caller's name and use it.
You mustn't ignore customers while you are on the phone.
You must smile and make eye contact if customers are waiting.
You must look after customers with specific needs.
You must be patient and helpful at all times.

■ Activity

Tell students they are going to practise giving instructions for a recipe. If necessary, revise important words and information needed. Divide the class into pairs, Student A and Student B. Direct them to the correct page for each role, reminding them not to look at the other student's information. Explain this is a two-stage pair activity. First, tell students to put the instructions for their recipes in the correct order by numbering the boxes. Go around the class, helping students where necessary. When they have finished, tell them to explain their recipe to their partner, who notes it down. Again, go around the class, helping where necessary. When both sets of instructions have been exchanged, tell students they can check the accuracy of the information they noted down. Go over general problems with the class, particularly any difficulties using sequence markers.

More words to use

Read the words aloud, asking students to repeat after you. Tell them to check any unfamiliar words in the Wordlist and learn them for homework.

Unit 16 Explaining and instructing

17 Taking telephone requests

- **Situations/functions**
  Replying to room service requests
  Describing facilities
- **Structures**
  need, *don't need*
- **Clothes, hotel facilities**

■ Revision of Unit 16

Expressions to learn
Ask students about kitchen and room servicing routines to elicit the expressions.

Revise *must*, *have to*, *don't have to*, and *mustn't* using these routines, hygiene regulations, and customer care maxims.

New words to use / More words to use
Recycle as suggested in Unit 2, using flashcards.

Other revision suggestions
- Tell students to do the Activity from Unit 16, working with a different partner.

■ Starter

Ask students what different services are offered by hotel housekeeping and room services. Tell students to look at the pictures, and ask them which hotel departments offer the services.

Answers

a room service	c room service
b housekeeping	d housekeeping

■ Listening *Room service. Can I help you?*

Draw students' attention to the first picture. Ask questions: *What's his job? Where is he? What is he doing? What's on his trolley? How many people are in the room? What have they ordered? How many glasses do they .... ?* Elicit: *glasses, champagne, need.* Draw students' attention to the second picture. Ask questions: *Who are the people in the picture? Where are they? What is the woman guest holding? Why is she giving them to the room attendant?* Elicit: *suit, dress, they need dry cleaning / ironing / repairing.* Draw students' attention to the third picture. Ask questions: *Who is in the room? What is he doing? What food is there? What kind of breakfast is it? Is it a cooked breakfast? Why did the guests order breakfast in their room?* Elicit: *continental breakfast, they need to leave soon.* Draw students' attention to the fourth picture. Ask questions: *Who is the man? Where is he? What is his problem? What do you think he's asking for?* Elicit: *zip, trousers, he needs a new zip.*

1. Tell students they are going to hear four calls made by guests with different requests. Ask students to tick the words they hear, and play the recording. Tell them to check their answers in pairs, and then go over the answers with the whole class.

Answers

    1 champagne, glasses
    2 dry cleaning, ironing
    3 breakfast, coffee
    4 zip, pressing

2. Ask students to predict the missing words in sentences 1–8. Play the recording again, and let students check their answers. Play the recording again section by section and go over the answers with the whole class.

Answers

    1 need
    2 needs
    3 ironing
    4 don't need
    5 long
    6 to leave
    7 them
    8 pressing

Ask students to turn to the Listening script on page 71. Model difficult and important phrases and structures, getting students to repeat chorally and individually. Ask students to practise the dialogues in pairs, swapping roles. Go around the class, monitoring and correcting. Note any areas causing difficulty and model these afterwards, asking students to repeat after you.

■ Language study

Expressions to learn
Ask students to read the expressions aloud, and check pronunciation and intonation. Ask them to learn the expressions for homework.

40 | Unit 17 Taking telephone requests

New words to use

Ask students to read the words aloud and check pronunciation. Tell them to check any unfamiliar words in the Wordlist and learn the new words for homework.

Structures to practise

need

Read through the examples of *need* + noun with the students. Explain that as a main verb, *need* is followed by a noun object. Read the example of *need* + *-ing* (gerund). Explain that, in the example, the dress is creased, so *it needs ironing*. If the dress isn't creased, *it doesn't need ironing*. Read the example of *need* + full infinitive. Point out that the negative form is *We don't need to ...* .

3 Tell students to read sentences 1–6 and then fill in the gaps. Go over the answers with the whole class.

Answers

1 need	3 doesn't need	5 don't need
2 need	4 needs	6 don't need

■ Listening *Facilities and services*

Tell students they are going to hear a hotel guest asking a receptionist about services. You could elicit or pre-teach some of the vocabulary by asking students what they would find near reception in a large international hotel: *foyer, lift/elevator, hairdressing salon, exchange bureau, coffee shop,* etc.

4 Ask students to read through questions 1–6. Check comprehension. Play the recording, pausing for students to refer to the questions and make notes. Let students check their answers in pairs. Play the recording again, pausing as each answer is given and go over the answers with the whole class.

Answers

1 change some money	5 he needs to change his plane ticket
2 in the foyer	
3 8.00a.m.–11.00p.m. every day	6 behind the lifts/elevators
4 on the other side of the foyer	

Ask students what nationality the guest is (American). Ask what the US English is for *lift* (*elevator*). Ask students if they know any more hotel/restaurant words that are different in US English: *bathroom = washroom* (US); *bill = check* (US); *foyer = lobby* (US); *head porter = bell captain* (US); *porter = bellboy* (US); *toilet = restroom* (US), etc.

5 Read through the lists of needs, and facilities and services with the students repeating after you. Check comprehension. Read the example sentences. Get students to practise making requests and responses in pairs using the information in the lists. Allow for a certain amount of creativity with students' answers.

■ Activity

Tell students they are going to practise taking requests over the phone. If necessary, revise important words and information needed. Divide the class into pairs, Student A and Student B, and sit them back-to-back. Direct them to the correct page for each role, reminding them not to look at the other student's information. When they have read the information, ask Student A (as the business traveller) to start by saying the example sentence: *Excuse me. I need to send a fax to Argentina.* Point out to Student B that they may be able to deal with some requests directly; others may need the help of another department in the hotel, such as Housekeeping or Room service. Remind students the roles are then reversed and Student A plays the part of the receptionist. Go around the class, helping students where necessary. When they have finished, go over general problems with the class, particularly any expressions you heard that were impolite or inappropriate.

More words to use

Ask the students to read the list of clothes aloud. Check pronunciation and comprehension. Read the names of the snack menu items, asking students to repeat after you. Tell them to check any unfamiliar words in the Wordlist. Ask them to learn the words for homework.

18 Taking difficult phone calls

- **Situations/functions**
  Asking for clarification over the phone
  Negotiating room rates
- **Structures**
  Past Simple: questions and short answers, negative statements
- **Spelling, telephone language**

■ Revision of Unit 17

Expressions to learn
Ask students to fill in the gaps using *need*, *don't need*, etc.
1 A bottle of champagne. Certainly, sir. How many glasses .... you .... ?
2 The bathroom is clean. You (not) .... do it.
3 Do the trousers .... pressing?
4 They .... leave early in the morning.
5 She (not) .... her jacket this afternoon.

New words to use
Recycle as suggested in Unit 2, using flashcards.

More words to use
Ask students to brainstorm the names of clothes. Ask them to name the items you find on a snack menu.

Other revision suggestions
- Ask students to describe some of the services and facilities found in a large, international hotel.
- Tell students to do the Activity from Unit 17, working with a different partner.

■ Starter
Draw students' attention to the Fidelio hotel reservations screen and get them to identify the seven pieces of information needed to make a room reservation.

Answers
arrival and departure dates, number of nights, number of adults, room type, contact name and number

■ Listening *Could you repeat that, please?*

1 Tell students they are going to listen to a phone dialogue between a reservations clerk and a man who wants to book accommodation. First, they have to identify the three pieces of information that Gabriella (the reservations clerk) can't hear. Play the recording. Go over the answers with the whole class.

Answers
Only *date*, *name*, and *telephone number* should be ticked.

2 Draw students' attention to the Fidelio screen. Tell them they must listen for the information to fill in the gaps, and play the recording. Let students check their answers in pairs. If necessary, play the recording again. Go over the answers with the whole class.

Answers
Arrival: September 4   Room Type: double
Nights: 3   Contact name: Alimoglu
Departure: September 7   Contact No.: +90 216 877 0343
Adults: 1

3 Explain to students that by putting the words in the correct order in 1–5, they will make the five sentences the reservations clerk says to get the information she needs. If necessary, do the first one as an example on the board. Let students check their sentences in pairs. Go over the answers with the whole class.

Answers
1 Can you speak up a little, please?
2 I'm sorry, I didn't catch the date.
3 Could you spell that for me?
4 Did you say N for November?
5 Could you repeat that, please?

Ask students to turn to the Listening script on page 71. Model and repeat difficult sentences and phrases, and get students to repeat after you chorally and individually. Students practise reading the dialogue back-to-back and in pairs, swapping roles. Go around and monitor their performance, helping where necessary. When students have practised enough, you could ask them to close their books and try to improvise the dialogue from memory.

Refer students to the Telephone alphabet on page 110. Tell them to work in pairs, and spell their own names for their partner: *My name's Garcia. That's G for Glove, A for Alpha, R for Romeo, C for Charlie, I for India, A for Alpha.*

■ Language study

Expressions to learn
Ask students to read the expressions aloud, and check their pronunciation and intonation. Ask them to learn the expressions for homework.

New words to use

Read the list of words with students repeating after you. Check comprehension by asking students what their *country code* is. Teach *less* as the opposite of *more*. *Standard room rate* is in contrast to *superior* or *executive room rate*. Tell them to check any unfamiliar words in the Wordlist and learn the new words for homework.

Structures to practise

Past Simple: questions and short answers

Explain that we make questions in the Past Simple with *did* and the base form of the verb. Draw students' attention to the examples in the book. Point out that the verb form *did* is the same with all persons.

4 Tell students to read the example sentences, and to make questions and short answers from sentences 1–6, answering *yes* or *no* as indicated in brackets. Go over the answers with the whole class.

Answers

1	Did they arrive last night?	Yes, they did.
2	Did he reserve two double rooms?	No, he didn't.
3	Did you hear what she said?	No, I didn't
4	Did Mr Alimoglu call from Istanbul?	Yes, he did.
5	Did she order a cooked breakfast?	Yes, she did.
6	Did you book a table for one o'clock?	No, I didn't.

Past Simple: negative statements

Explain that we make the negative Past Simple with *didn't* and the base form of the verb.

5 Ask students to look again at sentences 1–6 in exercise 4 and change them into the negative form. Go over the answers with the whole class.

Answers

1	They didn't arrive last night.	4	Mr Alimoglu didn't call from Istanbul.
2	He didn't reserve two double rooms.	5	She didn't order a cooked breakfast.
3	You didn't hear what she said.	6	You didn't book a table for one o'clock.

■ Listening *Negotiating room rates*

Read through the information in the table. Model the phrases and ask students to repeat after you so they will recognize them in the Listening. Tell students to check any unfamiliar words in the Wordlist.

6 Tell students they are going to hear a phone call between a woman customer and a reservations clerk. Explain that the missing information in the table is the price in euros. Tell students to complete the table as they listen, and play the recording. Let students check their answers in pairs. Play the recording again and go over the answers with the whole class.

Answers

1	€260 per night	3	€120 per night	5	€280
2	€200 per night	4	€320		

7 Tell students to read sentences 1–8, and predict the correct alternative. Ask them to check their answers as they listen, and play the recording. Go over the answers with the whole class.

Answers

1	double	3	give	5	too	7	less
2	discount	4	night	6	budget	8	weekend

Ask students to turn to the Listening script on page 71. Get them to practise reading the telephone dialogue in pairs, sitting back-to-back and swapping roles. Make a note of the problem areas and model these again afterwards, asking students to repeat after you. Suggest one pair performs the dialogue in front of the class.

■ Activity

Tell students they are going to practise asking for clarification over the phone. If necessary, revise important words and information needed. Divide the class into pairs, Student A and Student B, and sit them back-to-back. Direct them to the correct page for each role, reminding them not to look at the other student's information. When they have read the information, ask Student B to start by answering the phone: *Good morning. Windsor Hotel ...* . Go around the class, helping students where necessary. Encourage them to note down the important information. When both phone calls have finished, tell students to turn around and check the accuracy of the information they noted down. Go over general problems with the class, particularly any expressions you heard that were impolite or inappropriate.

More words to use

Read the list of telephone words, asking students to repeat after you. Tell students to check any unfamiliar words in the Wordlist and learn them for homework.

19 Health and safety at work

- **Situations/functions**
  Health and safety awareness
  Emergency procedures in a hotel
- **Structures**
  Adjectives and adverbs
- **Health and safety, emergency equipment**

Revision of Unit 18

Expressions to learn
Ask students to tell you what information a hotel needs to make a room reservation. Ask students for phrases to use on the telephone when the line is bad or the caller doesn't speak clearly.

New words to use / More words to use
Recycle as suggested in Unit 2, using flashcards. Divide into two different word groups: room rate and discount language; telephone language.

Other revision suggestions
- Get students to spell their names, street name, and home town using the Telephone alphabet on page 110.
- Re-elicit the rules for forming questions and negatives in the Past Simple.
- Get students to practise questions and short answers in the Past Simple.
- Tell students to do the Activity from Unit 18, working with a different partner.

Starter
Ask students to suggest possible health and safety hazards in hotel corridors and in kitchens. Ask them what emergency procedure there is in the building you are in. Ask how they know if there is a fire, and how they know what to do. Draw their attention to the pictures and tell them to find six health and safety hazards.

Answers
a	jumbled electrical cables, lack of protective gear
b	food stored with toxic chemicals (ketchup = tomato sauce)
c	oil/water on the floor
d	the hammer to break the glass is missing
e	the guard on the food slicer is open
f	the fire exit is blocked

Listening *Your health and safety is important to us*

A lot of the vocabulary in the Listening will be new to the students. Pre-teach the relevant words from New words to use. Also teach: *fire drill, first aider, food slicer, slip, bend, knees, strain* (your back). Model the pronunciation and get students to repeat after you so that they will recognize the words in the Listening.

1 Tell students they are going to hear a hotel health and safety officer instructing new personnel on basic health and safety rules and regulations. Ask students to read sentences 1–7. Tell students to mark them *true* or *false*, and play the recording. Let them check their answers in pairs. Play the recording again, pausing after each *true/false* topic. Go over the answers with the whole class. (Sentence 4 is *false* because staff should know the names of first aiders and find them at their jobs rather than waste time phoning reception.)

Answers
1	true
2	false
3	true
4	false
5	true
6	true
7	false

2 Read the five adverbs with students repeating after you. Check comprehension. Tell them to predict the correct adverbs in phrases 1–5. Play the recording and let them check their answers. Go over the answers with the whole class.

Answers
1	regularly
2	carefully
3	immediately
4	carefully
5	clearly

Language study

Expressions to learn
Ask students to read the expressions aloud, and check their pronunciation and intonation. Ask students to learn them for homework.

New words to use
Read the words aloud with students repeating after you. Tell them to check any words that are still unfamiliar in the Wordlist and learn the new words for homework.

Structures to practise

Adjectives and adverbs
Write on the board: *She's a **quick** reader. She reads **quickly**. / He's a **slow** writer. He writes **slowly**.* Check if the words in bold are adjectives or adverbs. (If students don't understand the terms, ask if the words in bold describe the noun or the verb.) Ask students to suggest a rule for making regular adverbs from adjectives (add -ly). Tell them to read the example sentences in the book. Point out the irregular adverbs: *well, hard, fast, late*.

3 Draw student's attention to the box of adjectives and adverbs. Check comprehension, and ask them to decide if each word is an adjective or an adverb. Ask students to complete sentences 1–8 with the correct word. Let them check their sentences in pairs. Go over the answers with the whole class.

Answers

1 fresh	3 serious	5 hard	7 late
2 carefully	4 quiet	6 expensive	8 politely

Listening *Sound the alarm!*

Ask what people should do if there is a fire; where they should go; what the name of the emergency service is that deals with fires; what equipment is usually on site to help deal with fires; and what an institution should do to make sure that all guests are accounted for (take a *roll call*).

4 Tell students they are going to hear an emergency situation in a hotel. Ask students to read questions 1–6. Check comprehension. Tell students to answer the questions as they listen, and play the recording. Let students check their answers in pairs, and play the recording again if necessary. Go over the answers with the whole class.

Answers

1 the fire alarm	4 she makes an announcement
2 in the kitchen	5 in front of the hotel
3 fire extinguishers	6 go to the assembly point and take a roll call, take the mobile with her

5 Ask students to read the list of safety regulations. Check comprehension. Ask students to tick the regulations done in the Listening, and play the recording. Let students check their answers in pairs. Go over the answers with the whole class.

Answers

All the regulations are done in the Listening except the second one: *Shut all the fire doors*.

Ask students to turn to the Listening script on page 72 and read the dialogue. Tell them to look up any words that are still unfamiliar in the Wordlist.

Activity

Tell students they are going to practise talking about health and safety at work. If necessary, revise important words and information needed. Divide the class into pairs and draw their attention to the safety hazard signs and the examples. Remind them they should discuss what the signs mean, and where you would find them in a hotel. Go around the class, helping students where necessary. When they have finished, tell them to check their answers on page 91. Go over general problems with the class.

More words to use
Ask students to repeat after you as you read through the different categories. Ask them to check any unfamiliar words in the Wordlist, and learn them for homework.

20 Giving directions indoors

- **Situations/functions**
  Directing guests around the hotel
- **Structures**
  Prepositions of location and direction
- **Bedrooms and bathrooms**

■ Revision of Unit 19

Expressions to learn

Ask questions and give prompts to elicit health and safety advice: *What should you do if you see an accident in the hotel? / You must keep the fire exits ....* Write the list of adverbs used in the Listening on the board: *carefully, clearly*, etc. and ask students to give you sentences using them.

New words to use / More words to use

Recycle as suggested in Unit 2, using flashcards.

Other revision suggestions

- Write a list of adjectives on the board (or say them). Ask students to give the corresponding adverbs (and make sentences with them).
- Brainstorm a list of emergency procedures in case of fire.
- Tell students to do the Activity from Unit 19, working with a different partner.

■ Starter

Draw students' attention to the plan of the hotel. Elicit the word *floor* from the students, and ask what the floor at street level is called. Explain that in British English this is called the *ground floor*. In US English, *ground floor = first floor*. Ask students to label parts 1–5 on the plan (in British English).

Answers

| 1 d | 2 c | 3 b | 4 a | 5 e |

■ Listening *Excuse me, where's the bar?*

Pre-teach: *turn right/left, it's on the right/left, it's in front of you, go through, go across, go past, at the top of, at the end of*. The preposition diagrams in the Structures to practise section will be useful here. Check that students understand the prepositions, and ask for examples using a preposition and a location in the hotel: *go into the shop, come out of the lift, walk along the corridor, at the end of the corridor, at the top/bottom of the stairs, go past the shop*, etc.

1 Tell students they are going to hear five dialogues in which a guest asks a member of the hotel staff for directions. Ask them to mark the five places on the plan as they listen. Give students the starting point before they hear each dialogue. The starting point for dialogues 1, 2, and 3 is on the ground floor near reception; for dialogues 3 and 4 it is somewhere on the first floor. Play the recording, pausing between each dialogue to remind them of the starting point of the next dialogue. Let students compare their answers in pairs. Play the recording again. Go over the answers with the whole class.

Answers

| 1 Room 102 | 3 Hotel shop | 5 Fitness centre |
| 2 Hair salon | 4 Conference suite A | |

2 Explain to students that phrases 1–8 are from the dialogues they have just heard. Ask them to complete the phrases as they listen, and play the recording. Let them check their answers in pairs. Play the recording again and go over the answers with the whole class.

Answers

1 Take	4 next to	7 through, past
2 along, on	5 turn	8 in front
3 across, end	6 past	

Ask students to turn to the Listening script on page 72 and read the dialogues. Model difficult and important phrases and structures, getting students to repeat chorally and individually. Students practise reading the dialogues in pairs, swapping roles. Go around and monitor their performance, helping where necessary. Make a note of any problem areas and model these again afterwards, with students repeating after you. When students have practised enough, you could ask them to close their books and try to improvise the dialogues from memory.

Language study

Expressions to learn

Ask students to read the expressions aloud and check pronunciation and intonation. Ask them to learn the expressions for homework.

New words to use

Ask students to read the words aloud and check pronunciation. (The phrase *turn-down service* means that the room attendent pulls the curtains and the folds back the bed spread in a guest's room, usually in the evening.) Tell them to check any unfamiliar words in the Wordlist and learn the list of words for homework.

Structures to practise

Prepositions of location and direction (1)

Draw students' attention to the preposition illustrations and ask them to give you more phrases using a preposition with an appropriate hotel location: **into** the bar, **out of** the lift, **along** the corridor, etc.

3 Tell students to look at the building plan and complete sentences 1–5 with one of the phrases or words given in the box. Ask them to compare answers in pairs. Go over answers with the whole class.

Answers

1 at the end of	3 past	5 at the bottom of
2 at the top of	4 out of	

4 Ask students to read the example, which gives directions from reception to Room 104. Ask them to follow the building plan and, working in pairs with the partner checking, give similar directions from reception to the places in 1–6.

Model answers

1. Take the lift to the second floor. Turn left out of the lift and it's at the end of the corridor.
2. Take the lift to the basement. Turn left out of the lift and go through the fitness centre. It's on the left.
3. Take the lift to the first floor. Go along the corridor and it's on the right.
4. Go across the lobby, and down the stairs to the basement. Turn right and it's on the right.
5. Take the lift to the third floor.
6. Take the lift to the first floor. Turn left out of the lift and it's on the right.

Listening *Is the room ready?*

Check if any of your students have worked as room attendants in hotels. Elicit what things have to be checked in each room after guests check out.

5 Draw students' attention to the picture of the hotel room. Ask students to work in pairs and match items 1–8 with the letters in the picture. Tell students they are going to listen to the housekeeper talking to a new room attendant and explaining her duties. Ask students to check their answers as they listen, and play the recording. Go over the answers with the whole class.

Answers

| 1 f | 2 g | 3 c | 4 a | 5 e | 6 h | 7 b | 8 d |

6 Tell students to read questions 1–6. Ask if they can predict the answers. Play the recording and let them check their answers. Play the recording again, pausing after each answer, and go over the answers with the whole class.

Answers

1 The hangers and spare bedding.	4 All the hotel information.
2 It isn't working.	5 Snacks and drinks.
3 Yes.	6 Pull the curtains and fold back the bedspread.

Activity

Tell students they are going to practise giving directions indoors. If necessary, revise important words and information needed. Divide the class into pairs: receptionist and hotel guest. Direct them to the plan of the ground floor of the Park Hotel on page 63. When they have looked at the plan, ask the student who is the guest to start by asking for directions. Point out it is helpful to start from Reception on the map. Remind students the roles are then reversed. Go around the class, helping students where necessary. When they have finished, go over general problems with the class, particularly any difficulties using prepositions.

More words to use

Read the words and ask students to repeat after you. Tell them to check any unfamiliar words in the Wordlist and learn them for homework.

Unit 20 Giving directions indoors | 47

21 Giving directions outside

- **Situations/functions**
  Asking for and giving directions outside
- **Structures**
  Prepositions of location and direction
- Street directions, the London Underground

■ Revision of Unit 20

Expressions to learn
Using the plan of the hotel on page 42, tell students to give you directions to different places, or tell you their location. If students are confident, you could also try this with the building you are in.

New words to use / More words to use
Ask students to name things they would find in: a hotel bedroom; a hotel bathroom.

Other revision suggestions
- Tell students to do the Activity from Unit 20, working with a different partner.

■ Starter
Check students know Lisbon is the capital of Portugal. Draw their attention to the tourist map of central Lisbon. Read some names of the locations marked on the map and ask students to say what kind of place they are, using the key to symbols. Ask them to read the list of places in the box, and find which ones are on the tourist map. Point out that *underground* and *metro* have the same meaning. (It is more common to refer to the *underground* in Britain; and the *metro* in mainland Europe.)

Answers
cinema, *hotel*, *railway station*, *theatre*, and *underground station* are all on the map.

■ Listening *Can you direct me to the theatre?*
Ask students to tell you the different ways of travelling in a city. Write on the board: *by train, by bus, by taxi, by metro*, etc. but *on foot*. You could also mention *on the underground* or *on the / by tube* (the conversational name for the London Underground system). Pre-teach the phrases: *quite near* (not as near as *near*), *the other side* (the side of the square opposite you), *you can't miss it* (it's very obvious).

1. Ask students to study the map. Give an unaccented pronunciation of the places that come up in the Listening: the *Dona Maria theatre* in *Rossio square*, the Roman museum (*Núcleo Arqueológico*) in *Rua dos Correeiros*, the *Oceanarium*. Point out the *Hotel International* and tell students they are going to hear reception staff giving three sets of directions to guests. Tell them to follow the directions on the map by drawing a line as they listen. Play the recording, pausing after each set of directions. Let students check in pairs that they have the same routes.

2. Tell students to look at the three sets of directions. Play the recording again, pausing after each section to give students time to complete the directions. Let students compare their answers in pairs. Play the recording again section by section, and go over the answers with the whole class.

Answers

Dialogue 1			
1 on foot	2 towards	3 on	
Dialogue 2			
4 outside	5 take	6 straight on	7 on
Dialogue 3			
8 take	9 Change	10 get off	

Ask students to turn to the Listening script on page 72. Model difficult and important phrases and structures, getting students to repeat chorally and individually. Students practise reading the dialogue in pairs, swapping roles. Give help where necessary. If students have difficulty with pronunciation and intonation, make a note of the problem areas and model these again afterwards, with students repeating after you.

When the students have practised enough, ask them to continue asking for and giving directions using a tourist map of a different city, preferably one in their country. (Have some copies available for them to use.)

■ Language study

Expressions to learn
Ask students to read the expressions aloud, and check their pronunciation and intonation. Ask them to learn the expressions for homework.

New words to use
Ask students to read the words aloud and check pronunciation. Tell them to check any unfamiliar words in the Wordlist and learn the list of words for homework.

Structures to practise

Prepositions of location and direction (2)

Draw students' attention to the preposition illustrations. Ask students to make sentences that give directions, using the prepositions: *Turn right **outside** the hotel. Go **under** / **over** the bridge. Get **off at** the first stop. Get **on at** Rossio. Walk **towards** the park. Go **straight on past** the theatre. Go **across** the square. Walk **up** / **down** the street **towards** the big office building*, etc. Point out that *on* and *off* are often used in connection with travelling by trains, buses, and planes.

3 Ask students to read sentences 1–6 and fill in the gaps with the most appropriate preposition from the list of words in the box. Let students compare their answers in pairs. Go over the answers with the whole class.

Answers

| 1 towards | 3 over, up | 5 off |
| 2 straight on | 4 outside | 6 across, on |

■ **Listening** *Travel in the city*

Ask students to study the map of the London Underground. Write the names on the board and practise the pronunciation of the stations they will hear mentioned in the Listening:

1 *Oxford Circus, Knightsbridge* /ˈnaɪtsbrɪdʒ/, *Green Park*. (*Harrods* is the name of a famous department store in Knightsbridge.)
2 *Embankment, Tower Hill*. Point out that the US English for *underground* or *metro* is *subway*.
3 *Charing Cross* /ˈtʃærɪŋ krɒs/, *Marble Arch, Tottenham Court Road* /ˈtɒtnəm kɔːt rəʊd/. (*The National Gallery* is a large picture gallery on Trafalgar Square.)
4 *Bond Street, Holborn* /ˈhəʊbən/, *King's Cross*.

Practise pronunciation of the underground lines in the key on the map, and ask students to find them.

4 Tell students they are going to hear four people asking directions. Tell them to find the starting point and the destination for each dialogue. Play the recording of the first set of directions. Let students compare their answers in pairs. Play the recording again. Go over the answers with the whole class. Repeat the procedure with dialogues 2, 3, and 4.

Answers

| 1 Oxford Circus to Knightsbridge | 3 Marble Arch to Charing Cross |
| 2 Leicester Square to Tower Hill | 4 Bond Street to King's Cross |

Ask students to turn to their Listening script on pages 72–3 and read the four dialogues. Model difficult and important phrases in the directions and get students to repeat after you chorally and individually. Students practise reading the dialogues in pairs, swapping roles. Go around and monitor their performance, helping where necessary. If students still have difficulty with pronunciation and intonation, make a note of the problem areas and model these again afterwards with students repeating after you.

5 Ask students to read the example. Give some starting points and destinations and elicit a few more examples of directions around the class. Tell students to continue practising in pairs, and to take turns asking for and giving directions.

■ **Activity**

Tell students they are going to practise giving directions outside. If necessary, revise important words and information needed. Divide the class into pairs, Student A and Student B. Direct them to the correct page for each role, reminding them not to look at the other student's information. When they have looked at the city street map and examples, ask Student A to start by asking for directions to the five places: *Excuse me. How do I get to …?* Point out they should start from Central Square on the map. Remind students the roles are then reversed, and Student A asks for directions to five different destinations. Go around the class, helping students where necessary. When they have finished, go over general problems with the class, particularly any difficulties with prepositions.

More words to use

Read the words, asking students to repeat after you. Tell them to check any unfamiliar words in the Wordlist and learn them for homework.

Unit 21 Giving directions outside

22 Facilities for the business traveller

▸ **Situations/functions**
Explaining hotel business facilities and services
▸ **Structures**
so, both ... and, but
▸ **Business and conference equipment**

■ Revision of Unit 21

Expressions to learn

Ask students to complete the sentences:

It's .... near here.
Turn right .... the hotel.
Walk .... the square.
It's on the .... of the square.
Keep straight on .... the street.
You .... miss it.

Refer students to the preposition diagrams in Unit 21 and ask them to make sentences using the prepositions.

New words to use

Recycle as suggested in Unit 2, using flashcards.

More words to use

Ask students to name the different forms of transport. Use pictures or drawings to revise road signs. Ask students to name as many street terms as they can.

Other revision suggestions

- Give starting places and destinations from the Lisbon or London Underground map. Ask students to give directions.
- Tell students to do the Activity from Unit 21, working with a different partner.

■ Starter

Check with students if the hotels they have worked in receive business travellers as well as tourists. Ask what differences there are between these two types of guest. Elicit from students some of the demands business travellers make: *high-speed Internet access, computers, printer, fax machine, video conferencing facilities, meeting rooms*. Ask students to look at the picture and name five pieces of office equipment.

Answers

> photocopier, personal computer, telephone, fax, printer

■ Listening *What can you offer the business traveller?*

Brainstorm as many in-room facilities and services as the class can think of. Write them on the board as a spidergram or mind map. Elicit as many items as possible of those listed in exercise 1. Give any that are missing. Go over all the items, modelling pronunciation, asking students to repeat after you. Check comprehension.

1 Tell students they are going to hear a dialogue between hotel reception and a customer enquiring about in-room facilities. Ask them to tick all the items mentioned in the dialogue, and play the recording. Let students compare their answers in pairs. Play the recording again and go over the answers with the whole class.

Answers

> All the facilities or services should be ticked, except *disabled access, garden, swimming pool*, and *laundry service*.

Ask students which of these are mainly for the business traveller.

Answers

> photocopier, multi-line phones, broadband, printer, fax, emails

2 Tell students to look at sentences 1–6. Ask if they can predict the missing words using the list in exercise 1. Ask students to check and correct their answers as they listen, and play the recording. Go over the answers with the whole class.

Answers

> 1 pay-per-view   3 electronic safe   5 photocopier, fax
> 2 emails   4 24-hour   6 broadband

■ Language study

Expressions to learn

Ask students to read the expressions aloud, and check their pronunciation and intonation. Ask students to learn the expressions for homework.

50   Unit 22 Facilities for the business traveller

New words to use

Read the list of words with students repeating after you. Repeat any that cause difficulty. Tell them to check any unfamiliar words in the Wordlist. Ask students to learn the list of words for homework.

Structures to practise

Linking and contrasting

so, both ... and, but

Tell students spoken English and written English style is often improved by linking short sentences together to make a longer sentence. Draw students' attention to the example sentences. Read them through with the students. Point out we use *so* when we give a reason for something; *both ... and* when two things have the same qualities; *but* when the information is contrasting. Give more simple examples around the class and ask students to link the sentences: *The door is closed. You can't hear the noise in the corridor.* (so) / *You have a book. I have a book.* (both ... and) / *It's raining. The students are going to play football.* (but)

3 Ask students to read sentences 1–6 and use *so, both ... and,* or *but* to link them. Let students compare their answers in pairs. Go over the answers with the whole class.

Answers

1 The hair salon is open during the week but it's closed at weekends.
2 The restaurant is fully booked so we can't take any more bookings.
3 Both the hotel and leisure centre have fitness centres.
4 The chef is ill so the sous chef is in charge.
5 The table was booked for eight o'clock but the guests didn't arrive until 9.00.
6 Both Petra and Dirk finish their work placements next week.

■ **Listening** *We're planning a conference*

Check if any students have ever been involved with conference planning. Elicit some of the needs of a large conference: *meeting rooms, microphones, projectors, screens, PowerPoint facilities, secretarial services.* (*PowerPoint is the computer graphics package used for presentations.*)

4 Tell students they are going to hear a customer enquiring about a hotel's conference facilities. Ask students to read the list of rooms and equipment, and predict the answers by matching them with the pictures. Play the recording and let students check their answers.

Answers

1 b   2 a   3 d   4 c

5 Explain to students that they have to complete the table of conference facilities with the information in the recording. Elicit what information students already know (the type of rooms), and let them fill in that part of the table. Ask students to listen for the missing information, and play the recording. Elicit the answers around the class and write them on the board. It may be worth pointing out that a digital projector used for PowerPoint presentations is commonly known as a *beamer*. Model pronunciation of the words and phrases, asking students to repeat after you.

Answers

type of rooms: theatre-style, boardroom-style, classroom-style, banqueting
type of audio visual equipment: digital projectors, slide projectors, screens, PowerPoint facilities
business services: high-speed data lines (broadband), full secretarial services, video-conferencing

■ **Activity**

Tell students they are going to practise taking a booking for a business conference over the phone. If necessary, revise important words and information needed. Divide the class into pairs, Student A and Student B, and sit them back-to-back. Direct them to the correct page for each role, reminding them not to look at the other student's information. When they have read the information, ask Student B to start by taking a booking for a business conference: *Hello. Hotel Olympia. Can I help you?* Go around the class, helping students where necessary. Encourage them to note down the important information. When both phone calls have finished, tell students they can turn around and check the accuracy of the information they noted down. Go over general problems with the class, particularly any expressions you heard that were impolite or inappropriate.

More words to use

Read the lists of words and phrases, asking students to repeat after you. Tell students to check any unfamiliar words in the Wordlist and learn them for homework.

23 Offering help and advice

→ **Situations/functions**
Giving help and advice

→ **Structures**
Present Perfect
should

→ **Illness and first aid**

■ Revision of Unit 22

Expressions to learn

Ask students to tell you how a guest asks about in-room facilities, and facilities for business travellers; and how a member of staff would reply.

New words to use / More words to use

Ask students to tell you all the in-room facilities they can remember, and which ones are more useful for business travellers. Tell students to brainstorm conference facilities into three categories: rooms, equipment, and services. Prepare flashcards for this vocabulary revision, as suggested in Unit 2.

Other revision suggestions

- Get students to give you different sentences using the linkers: *so, both ... and, but*.
- Tell students to do the Activity from Unit 22, working with a different partner.

■ Starter

Check if students have ever had to offer guests help and advice in their work. Draw their attention to the photographs. Ask students to tell you where each photograph is and who they can see. Ask what they think has happened to the male guest (he has fainted and hit his head).

■ Listening *Emergency first aid needed*

Continue eliciting the story in the photographs from the students, helping with vocabulary. Pre-teach: *fallen over, hit his head, fainted, How are you feeling?, Are you in pain?, plaster, bleeding, ambulance*. Tell students to follow the story in the photographs as they listen, and play the recording.

1   Ask students to read sentences 1–6. Check comprehension. Tell students to work in pairs and answer as many as they can from memory. Let students check their answers, and play the recording again. Go over the answers with the whole class.

Answers

| 1 false | 2 true | 3 true | 4 false | 5 true | 6 false |

2   Ask students to look at sentences 1–6. Tell them to try to predict the missing words. Play the recording, pausing for students to complete the sentences. Let students compare their answers in pairs. Play the recording again, and go over the answers with the whole class.

Answers

| 1 has just fallen | 3 haven't had | 5 we've called |
| 2 Don't | 4 should | 6 cut |

Ask students to turn to the Listening script on page 73. Model difficult and important phrases and structures, especially those where advice is offered. Get students to repeat chorally and individually. Students practise reading the dialogue in groups of three, swapping roles. Go around and their monitor performance, helping where necessary. Suggest one or two groups perform the dialogue in front of the class.

■ Language study

Expressions to learn

Ask students to read the expressions aloud, and check pronunciation and intonation. Ask them to learn the expressions for homework.

New words to use

Read the words aloud with students repeating after you. Tell them to check any unfamiliar words in the Wordlist. Ask students to learn the new words for homework.

Structures to practise

Present Perfect

Read through the explanation of the Present Perfect, and the frequent use of *just* and *yet* with the tense. Read through the example sentences with the students. Explain that we use the Present Perfect with *just* for actions which have only recently finished. Give examples: *I've just bought a new car.* (*I bought it yesterday*), etc. Ask students to give more examples. Explain that we use the Present Perfect with *yet* when we talk about an action that has not yet happened but we expect to happen in the future. Give examples: *I lost my bag yesterday. I haven't found it yet* (*but I'm still looking*), etc. Ask students to give more examples.

3 Ask students to complete sentences 1–6 by putting the verbs into the Present Perfect. Let students compare their answers in pairs before you go over them with the whole class.

Answers

1 The Japanese group has just arrived.
2 I haven't finished my exercise yet.
3 The man has had a bad fall.
4 They haven't eaten lunch yet.
5 We have lived here all our lives.
6 He hasn't started work yet.

Giving advice

should

Read the example sentences with the students. Explain that *should* and *shouldn't* are used for giving advice about the best action to take in a situation.

4 Tell students to read sentences 1–6 and the advice in sentences a–f. Check comprehension. Ask them to work in pairs to match each situation with a piece of advice. Go over the answers with the whole class.

Answers

1 d   2 a   3 f   4 b   5 c   6 e

■ **Listening** *Can you call a doctor, please?*

5 Tell students they are going to hear four dialogues where first aid or medical help is needed. Tell them to note down the problem and the action in their books. Play the recording, pausing after each dialogue so that students can write their notes. Let students compare their answers in pairs. Play the recording again, pausing after each dialogue and go over the answers with the whole class.

Answers

Problem	Action
1 boy is hot and sick	call the doctor
2 wife has toothache	emergency dentist's number, pharmacy across the road
3 waiter has burnt his hand	put his hand in cold water
4 guest has fallen down the stairs	call an ambulance and a first aider

6 Ask students to turn to the Listening script on page 73. Model difficult and important phrases and structures. Get students to repeat chorally and individually. Students practise reading the dialogue in pairs, swapping roles. Go around and monitor their performance, helping where necessary.

■ **Activity**

Tell students they are going to practise giving help and advice after an accident. If necessary, revise important words and information needed. Divide the class into pairs. Draw their attention to the description of the accident and the list of actions. Explain this is a two-stage pair activity. First, tell students to decide which actions they should do and which they shouldn't do. Go around the class, helping students where necessary. When they have finished, tell them to number the actions they **should** do in order of importance. When they have finished both tasks, you could compare and discuss the answers of different pairs. Finally, go over general problems with the class, particularly any difficulties using *should* and *shouldn't*.

More words to use

Ask students to repeat after you as you read through the different categories. Ask them to check any unfamiliar words in the Wordlist and learn them for homework.

24 Dealing with problems

→ **Situations/functions**
Making complaints
Giving explanations and solutions

→ **Structures**
should + Present Perfect Passive

→ **Topics for complaints**

■ **Revision of Unit 23**

Expressions to learn
Elicit answers for the questions about this situation:
A guest has just fallen badly. What should you do? What questions would you ask him or her? What advice would you give him or her?

New words to use
Recycle as suggested in Unit 2, using flashcards.

More words to use
Brainstorm health problems and healthcare personnel.

Other revision suggestions
- Ask students the names of the three emergency services.
- Ask students to give you examples of things they have *just* done or haven't done *yet*, using the Present Perfect.
- Tell students to do the Activity from Unit 23, working with a different partner.

■ **Starter**

Draw students' attention to pictures a–f. Read the list of problems 1–6 with students repeating after you. Check comprehension. Ask students to match the problems with the pictures.

Answers

| 1 c | 2 d | 3 a | 4 e | 5 f | 6 b |

■ **Listening** *Are we service-minded enough?*

Ask students what they think should have been done by staff in the situations in the pictures. Elicit: *service engineer* (for air-conditioning), *maintenance* (for shower).

1   Tell students they are going to hear six dialogues of hotel guests complaining to staff about the service. Ask students to read problems 1–6 again from the Starter and solutions a–f from exercise 1. Tell them to predict the solutions to the problems. Play the recording, pausing after each dialogue so students can check their answers. Play the recording again, and go over the answers with the whole class.

Answers

| a 5 | b 4 | c 6 | d 3 | e 1 | f 2 |

2   Ask students to read sentences 1–6 and predict the missing words. Play the recording, pausing after each dialogue while students check and correct their sentences. Let students compare their answers in pairs. Play the recording again, and go over the answers with the whole class.

Answers

| 1 requested | 3 made | 5 have had |
| 2 have been | 4 should have been | 6 hasn't been |

Ask students to turn to the Listening script on page 73. Model difficult and important phrases and structures, especially the staff responses to the complaints, getting students to repeat chorally and individually. Students practise reading the dialogues in pairs, swapping roles. Go around and monitor their performance, helping where necessary. If the students have difficulty with pronunciation and intonation, make a note of the problem areas and model these again afterwards, with students repeating after you. When students have practised enough, you could ask them to close their books and try to improvise the dialogues from memory.

■ **Language study**

Expressions to learn
Ask students to read the expressions aloud, and check their pronunciation and intonation. Ask them to learn the expressions for homework.

New words to use
Ask students to read the words aloud and check pronunciation. Tell them to check any unfamiliar words in the Wordlist. Ask the class to learn them for homework.

Structures to practise

should + Present Perfect Passive

Draw students' attention to pictures b and e again. Point out hotel rooms are serviced every day. Read the first example sentence: *The room **should have been cleaned**.* Point out the man asked for the overnight laundry service. Read the second example sentence: *The shirts **should have been delivered**.* Give students other situations of bad service to elicit the *should have been* construction: *The shower's still broken. / The bathroom's dirty. / Reception haven't given the message. / The drinks haven't been served*, etc.

3 Tell students to read the example sentences and ask them to write responses to problems 1–6 in the same way. Let students compare their answers in pairs. Go over the answers with the whole class.

Answers

1 It should have been replaced.
2 It should have been cleaned.
3 It should have been emptied.
4 They should have been washed.
5 It should have been mended.
6 It should have been ordered.

4 Tell students they have to acknowledge the problem and also offer some kind of solution or response to the guest. Go through the exercise sentence by sentence, giving help where necessary and ask students to write the answers. Check, correct, and write good models on the board.

Model answers

1 I'm sorry, it should have been cleaned. I'll send someone up immediately.
2 I'm sorry, the drinks should have been replaced. I'll send someone up immediately.
3 I'm sorry, they should have been replaced. I'll send some up immediately.
4 I'm sorry, you should have been given a quieter room. I'll change your room immediately.
5 I'm sorry, it should have been checked this morning. I'll send someone up immediately.
6 I'm sorry, your order should have arrived by now. I'll look into it.

Get students to practise saying the responses around the class, repeating after you if necessary. Check their intonation and make sure the apologies sound apologetic. Tell students to continue practising the problems and responses in pairs, swapping roles.

■ Listening *Did you enjoy your stay?*

Tell students they are going to hear a follow-up phone call from a hotel to a recent guest who complained about the service. Pre-teach: *properly, wheelchair, complimentary*.

5 Tell students to read sentence pairs 1–6. They may already be able to tell you some of the correct statements. Ask them to tick the correct statements as they listen, and play the recording. Let students compare their answers in pairs. Play the recording again, pausing after each statement and go over the answers with the whole class.

Answers

1 Personnel called Mrs White about a complaint.
2 The hotel had good wheelchair access.
3 The first room wasn't on the ground floor.
4 It was too noisy.
5 The second room was quiet and near the garden.
6 The manager sent flowers and champagne.

6 Tell students to turn to the Listening script on pages 73–4. Model difficult and important phrases and structures, getting students to repeat chorally and individually. Students practise reading the dialogues in pairs, swapping roles. Go around and monitor their performance, helping where necessary. If the students have difficulty with pronunciation and intonation, make a note of the problem areas and model these again afterwards, with students repeating after you.

■ Activity

Tell students they are going to practise dealing with a complaint. If necessary, revise important words and information needed. Divide the class into pairs. Draw their attention to the extract from a letter of complaint to a hotel, and the example. When they have read the extract, ask them to discuss the letter and offer advice and solutions for each of the complaints. Go around the class, helping students where necessary. When they have finished, go over general problems with the class, particularly any difficulties using *should* + Present Perfect Passive.

More words to use

Read the words, asking students to repeat after you. Tell them to check any unfamiliar words in the Wordlist and learn them for homework.

25 Paying bills

- **Situations/functions**
  Taking payments
- **Structures**
  Present Continuous
  Object pronouns
- **Payment methods**

■ Revision of Unit 24

Expressions to learn
Give prompts to revise typical complaints made by hotel guests: *smoky room / dirty bathroom / broken TV / broken light bulb / long wait for room service / taxi hasn't arrived*, etc. Revise staff responses: apologies, what should have been done, and a solution or action.

New words to use / More words to use
Recycle as suggested in Unit 2, using flashcards.

Other revision suggestions
- Tell students to do the Activity from Unit 24, working with a different partner.

■ Starter
Check if students have had any experience of handling bills at work. Ask them to think of some ways in which guests usually pay, and what currencies and cards are widely used.

■ Listening *Could we have our bill, please?*

1 Tell students they are going to hear two dialogues of people paying bills. Draw their attention to the two screens. Elicit or teach *value added tax* (VAT), *service*, *Visa slip, receipt, cash, total* and check pronunciation of these items. You could also point out that *beverage* (screen a) is another word for drink. Ask students to match the dialogues to the correct screen, and play the recording. Go over the answers with the whole class.

Answers
1 a   2 b

2 Ask students to read through questions 1–7. Check comprehension. Play the recording and ask students to note the answers to the questions. Go over the answers with the whole class.

Answers
1 yes	3 now	5 no	7 no
2 with Visa	4 yes	6 in cash	

Ask students to turn to the Listening script on page 74. Model difficult and important phrases and structures, getting students to repeat chorally and individually. Students practise reading the dialogues in pairs, swapping roles. Give help where necessary. If students have difficulty with pronunciation and intonation, make a note of the problem areas and model these again afterwards, asking students to repeat after you.

■ Language study

Expressions to learn
Ask students to read the expressions aloud, and check pronunciation and intonation. Ask them to learn the expressions for homework.

New words to use
Ask students to read the words aloud and check pronunciation. Tell them to check any unfamiliar words in the Wordlist. Ask the class to learn the list of words for homework.

Structures to practise
Present Continuous

Explain that there are two present tenses in English: Present Simple, for something that happens regularly: *We walk to college. We go to lessons*, etc; and Present Continuous to describe something that is happening at the time of speaking: *You're sitting in the classroom. He's wearing a blue jacket*, etc. Point out the Present Continuous is made with *am / are / is + -ing*. Give students some examples of negatives and question forms: *They aren't coming today. She isn't listening to me. Are you enjoying your week? Is he writing the answers?* If your students are confident, you could explain the spelling rules governing the formation of the *-ing* form at this point. Write them on the board in three groups:

go–going, drink–drinking, etc.   (Add *-ing*.)
come–coming, serve–serving, etc.   (Remove *-e* and add *-ing*.)
sit–sitting, cut–cutting, etc.   (Double the consonant and add *-ing*.)

Ask students to add more words to the lists and see if they can work out the spelling rules for themselves.

3 Read questions 1–6 and ask students to answer the questions orally around the class. Tell students to continue asking and answering each other in pairs. If you feel they need more practice, ask students to describe what is happening in some of the photographs in their books: pages 14, 32, 34, 48.

Object pronouns

Ask students to read the two example sentences from the restaurant dialogue in the first Listening. Explain that *us* replaces the names of the guests and *them* replaces the drinks, and that these are the objects of the verbs in the sentences. Ask students to look at the list of object pronouns, and give them a few moments to memorize them. Then tell them to close their books and call out the subject pronouns (*I, you, he, she*, etc.). Ask students to give the corresponding object pronoun.

4 Tell students to read sentence pairs 1–6. Ask them to complete the sentences with the correct object pronoun. Let students compare their answers in pairs. Go over the answers with the whole class.

Answers

| 1 it | 2 them | 3 her | 4 him | 5 us | 6 you |

■ Listening How would you like to pay?

5 Tell students they are going to hear four dialogues of different payment situations. Pre-teach: *invoice, extras, voucher, traveller's cheques, change*. Ask students to write the correct methods of payment as they listen, and play the recording, pausing after each dialogue. Let students compare their answers in pairs. Play the recording again, and go over the answers with the whole class.

Answers

| 1 with Mastercard | 3 by credit card (Visa) |
| 2 with US dollar traveller's cheques | 4 in cash |

6 Ask students to read sentences 1–4. Check comprehension. Ask them to mark the sentences *true* or *false* as they listen, and play the recording. Let students check their answers in pairs. Go over the answers with the whole class, playing the recording again if necessary.

Answers

| 1 false | 2 true | 3 true | 4 false |

Ask students to turn to the Listening script on page 74 and read the four dialogues. Model difficult and important phrases and get students to repeat after you chorally and individually. Students practise reading the dialogues in pairs, swapping roles. Go around and monitor their performance, helping where necessary. If students still have difficulty with pronunciation and intonation, make a note of the problem areas and model these again, asking students to repeat after you.

■ Activity

Tell students they are going to practise taking bill payments. If necessary, revise important words and information needed. Divide the class into pairs, Student A and Student B. Draw their attention to the five situations for paying a bill and the example.

When they have read the information, ask Student A (as the customer) to choose a different method of payment for each situation and the amount (if any) of the tip. Ask Student B (as the member of staff) to decide the amount for each bill and the extras included. Then ask Student A to start by asking: *Excuse me. Could I have the bill now, please?* Go around the class, helping students where necessary. Remind students the roles are then reversed, and Student A is the member of staff. Give them time to change the methods of payment, the amounts, the tip (if any), and the extras included. Again, go around helping where necessary. When they have finished, go over general problems with the class, particularly any suggestions you heard that were impolite or inappropriate.

More words to use

Read the lists with students repeating after you. Distinguish between *credit* and *debit cards*: credit card bills are paid by customers every month; debit card payments come directly from customers' bank accounts. Check pronunciation and comprehension. Ask them to learn the lists for homework.

26 Payment queries

Situations/functions
Handling queries politely

Structures
much, many, a lot of

Payment procedure

Revision of Unit 25

Expressions to learn
Ask students to complete the sentences:

I asked for my bill to be ....
It's ready ....
How .... you .... to pay?
.... you sign here, please?
Is service .... ?
How .... you paying?
The .... in euros is just here.
Would you like a VAT .... ?

New words to use
Ask students to name possible methods of payment. Recycle as suggested in Unit 2, using flashcards.

More words to use
Ask students to name some different credit and debit cards. Give them the names of countries and ask them to name the currencies.

Other revision suggestions
- Ask students to tell you what they're doing, reading, sitting on, studying, wearing, etc.
- Ask students to substitute an object pronoun for an object noun: *I saw **the manager** yesterday.* (him) / *She paid **the bill** and said goodbye.* (it) / *I gave **the girls** the message.* (them)
- Tell students to do the Activity from Unit 25, working with a different partner.

Starter
Again, check if any of your students have had experience handling payments at work. Ask what some frequent reasons for queries over hotel and restaurant bills are. Tell students to look at the two pictures. Ask them what problems they think these customers are having with their bills.

Answers
a the customer has received the wrong bill (of the table behind her)
b the man has received a big bill for his son's use of the phone and minibar

Listening *I think there's a mistake*
Tell students they are going to listen to two customers querying their bills, the first in a restaurant and the second in a hotel.

1 Ask students to read through sentences 1–3. Check comprehension. Tell students to mark the sentences *true* or *false* as they listen, and play Dialogue 1. Let students compare their answers. Play the recording again and go over the answers with the whole class. Repeat the procedure for sentences 4–6 and Dialogue 2.

Answers
| 1 true | 2 true | 3 false | 4 false | 5 true | 6 true |

2 Tell students to read sentences 1–6. Ask them to complete the sentences as they listen, and play the recording. Let students compare their answers in pairs. Play the recording again and go over the answers with the whole class.

Answers
| 1 mistake | 3 much | 5 many |
| 2 lot of | 4 much | 6 didn't |

Ask students to turn to the Listening script on page 74 and read the dialogues. Model difficult and important phrases and get students to repeat after you chorally and individually. Students practise reading the dialogues in pairs, swapping roles. Go around and monitor their performance, helping where necessary. If students still have difficulty with pronunciation and intonation, make a note of the problem areas and model these again afterwards, asking students to repeat after you. When students have practised enough, you could ask them to close their books and try to improvise the dialogues from memory.

Language study

Expressions to learn

Ask students to read the expressions aloud, and check their pronunciation and intonation. Ask students to learn the expressions for homework.

New words to use

Ask students to read the words aloud and check pronunciation. Tell them to check any unfamiliar words in the Wordlist. Ask the class to learn the list of words for homework.

Structures to practise

much, many, a lot of

Write *much* on the board. Read the first two example sentences and explain that we use *much* with uncountable nouns in questions and negative sentences. Do the same procedure with *many* and explain its use with countable nouns. Call out countable and uncountable nouns: *rooms, time,* etc. Ask students to respond with a sentence: *There aren't many rooms. There isn't much time,* etc. Follow this with a similar drill to elicit question forms: *Is there much time? Are there many rooms? How many glasses? How much money?* etc.

Write *a lot of* on the board. Read the example sentences and explain that it can be used in all cases with countable and uncountable nouns, except with the question word *How*. Elicit more examples from students using *There is/There isn't a lot of…, There are/aren't a lot of…, Is there/Are there a lot of…?* etc.

3 Ask students to read sentences 1–8. Tell them to consider whether the sentences are positive, negative, or a question; and whether the noun is countable or uncountable. Ask students to complete the sentences and compare their answers in pairs. Go over the answers with whole class.

Answers

1 many/a lot of	4 much/a lot of	7 a lot of
2 a lot of	5 a lot of	8 much
3 many	6 much/a lot of	

Listening *Working with Fidelio Suite 7*

Draw students' attention to the five small screens. Ask them what procedure they think is shown.

4 Tell students they are going to hear how to check out one of the hotel guests, *Mr Rodrigues*. Ask them to read questions 1–3. Check comprehension. Tell them to choose the correct alternative as they listen, and play the recording.

Answers

| 1 Fidelio | 2 creating an invoice | 3 at reception |

5 Ask students to read the dialogue and put the sentences in the correct order using numbers. Play the recording again and let them check and correct their answers. Go over the answers with the whole class.

Answers

1 First, look at the guest list …	4 He's paying by Visa …
2 Then click on the guest's name …	5 Now, his charges all appear …
3 All the items for his bill …	6 You've just checked out a guest.

Activity

Tell students they are going to practise dealing with payment queries. If necessary, revise important words and information needed. Divide the class into pairs, Student A and Student B. Direct them to the correct page for each role, reminding them not to look at the other student's information. When they have read the information and examples, ask Student A (as the guest) to start by saying: *Excuse me, but there's been a mistake …* . Go around the class, helping students where necessary. Remind students the roles are then reversed, and Student A is the member of staff. When they have finished, go over problems with the class, particularly examples of forgetting to apologize or expressions you heard that were impolite or inappropriate.

More words to use

Read the lists of words and phrases, asking students to repeat after you. Tell students to check any unfamiliar words in the Wordlist and learn them for homework.

Unit 26 Payment queries

27 Applying for a job

- **Situations/functions**
  Writing a CV
  Answering a job advertisement
- **Structures**
  Formal language for business letters and applications
- **Job advertisements**

Revision of Unit 26

Expressions to learn

Ask students how customers ask for their bills in a restaurant; and in a hotel. Ask how a customer would point out a mistake; and how a member of staff would apologize for giving a customer the wrong bill.

New words to use / More words to use

Ask students to brainstorm all the payment words, or recycle as suggested in Unit 2, using flashcards.

Other revision suggestions

- Ask students to complete the sentences with *much*, *many*, or *a lot of*:
  1 Are there .... suites in the hotel?
  2 I have .... work to do tomorrow.
  3 They saw .... people in the bar.
  4 We don't have .... time.
  5 There aren't .... customers here tonight.
- Ask students to tell you the correct sequence of the Fidelio checkout procedure.
- Tell students to do the Activity from Unit 26, working with a different partner.

Starter

Students may have already written a CV of their own but explain this is a good opportunity to update and improve it. Ask students to brainstorm in pairs the most important things to include on a CV. Get them to look at the partially completed CV of Caroline Davros and compare it with their ideas. Check comprehension. Model important or difficult words and phrases and get students to repeat after you.

Listening *Writing your CV*

1 Tell students they are going to hear Caroline Davros registering at a job agency. Elicit examples of what type of information is missing on her CV. Ask students to complete the CV as they listen, and play the recording, pausing after each piece of missing information. Let students compare their answers in pairs. Play the recording a second time and, if necessary, a third time. Go over the answers with the whole class.

Answers

Qualifications:	baccalaureate professionale, BEP in Tourism and Hospitality
Work experience:	Hotel Central, Geneva; Receptionist Sun Hotel, Receptionist Sofitel, Receptionist
Personal qualities:	sociable, friendly, enjoys helping and advising people, well organized, hard-working
References:	Manager, Sofitel

2 Read the example sentences and continue asking students questions about their qualifications, work experience, and personal qualities around the class. Tell students to work in pairs as Caroline and the agent, asking and answering questions, swapping roles. Go around and monitor their performance, helping and correcting as necessary.

Language study

Expressions to learn

Ask students to read the expressions aloud, and check their pronunciation and intonation. Ask where they would find these expressions (in a formal letter of application). Point out that **A** after each expression stands for *applicant*. Explain that you use the beginning *Dear Sir/Madam* when you don't know the name of the person you are writing to. The ending for these letters is *Yours faithfully*. If necessary, revise the difference between *Mr* (for all men), *Mrs* (for married women), *Miss* (for unmarried women) and *Ms* (for all women. This is now often preferred by married and unmarried women, and certainly to be used if in doubt). The ending for letters that begin with a name is *Yours sincerely*. Ask students to learn the expressions for homework.

Unit 27 Applying for a job

New words to use

Read the words aloud, asking students to repeat after you. Tell them to check any unfamiliar words in the Wordlist. Ask students to learn them for homework.

Structures to practise

Formal language for business letters and applications

3 Tell students to look at the application letter with the missing words and phrases and to choose the most suitable expressions from Expressions to learn to complete the letter. Let students compare their answers in pairs. Go over the letter with the whole class.

Answer

> 1 Sir/Madam
> 2 I would like to apply for
> 3 Would you please send me
> 4 enclose

■ Listening *Writing a covering letter*

Check if students have ever written a covering letter to go with a job application. Ask what sort of information they included. Tell them that they are going to hear a young man (Michel) from Lyon in France giving biographical information about himself. Elicit or pre-teach: *catering college, cooking skills, own apartment, clean driving licence.*

4 Ask students to look at the biographical information they have to listen for. Tell them to complete the form as they listen, and play the recording. Let students compare their answers in pairs. Play the recording again, and go over the answers with the whole class.

Answers

> Name: Michel Laval
> Age: 21
> Professional qualifications: chef's certificate
> Work experience: experience in various hotels and restaurants while training
> Current job: in Grand Hotel Mercure in Lyon
> Reasons for answering advert: wants more responsibility and to use cooking skills more.

5 Draw students' attention to the job advertisement. Explain that *Michelin Red M* is a recognized chef's qualification. Point out that accommodation is not provided, and the applicant must have his or her own transport. Ask students if they think it would be a suitable job for Michel Laval. Play the recording from exercise 4 again, and let students note down any more details which would be relevant to an application.

Ask students to read the covering letter on page 88, and draw their attention to the key phrases and formal language structures in bold.

Tell students to work in pairs and write a covering letter to go with Michel's application for the position of junior sous chef. Monitor as they write, and help or correct as necessary.

Model answer

> Dear Mr Lescaux
> I am writing to apply for the position of junior sous chef.
> I am a fully trained chef with a chef's certificate, and I have experience working in various hotels and restaurant kitchens as a kitchen porter and commis chef. I currently work at the Grand Hotel Mercure in the centre of Lyon.
> I would like to apply for the position advertised as I would really like to have more responsibility and use my cooking skills more. I am sociable, and I have my own apartment in Lyon, and a clean driving licence.
> I enclose a copy of my CV. I look forward to hearing from you.
> Yours sincerely
> Michel Laval

■ Activity

Tell students they are going to practise giving biographical information about themselves. If necessary, revise important words and information needed. Divide the class into pairs, Student A and Student B. Explain this is a two-stage pair activity. First, tell students to write a short biography about themselves, inventing some qualifications and work experience. Go around the class, helping students where necessary. When they have finished, draw their attention to the example dialogue and ask Student A to start (as the interviewer) by asking: *What professional qualifications do you have?* Again, go around helping where necessary. Encourage them to note down the important information. Remind students the roles are then reversed, and Student A is the applicant. Finally, go over general problems with the class, particularly any difficulties asking appropriate questions and giving full answers.

More words to use

Ask students to repeat after you as you read through the two lists. Check comprehension and ask them to learn the lists for homework.

28 The interview

- **Situations/functions**
  A job interview
- **Structures**
  Talking about the future
- **Career, interview tips**

■ **Revision of Unit 27**

Expressions to learn

Get students to tell you the beginnings and endings of business letters. Ask them for the phrases for a letter answering a job advertisement.

New words to use / More words to use

Recycle as suggested in Unit 2, using flashcards.

Other revision suggestions:
- Ask students to tell you the essential information needed on a CV.
- Tell students to do the Activity from Unit 27, working with a different partner.

■ **Starter**

Draw students' attention to the picture. Explain that this is a group of young people just starting out on their careers. Ask students to give you some adjectives to describe them (*smart, happy, confident, positive*). Introduce the job interview as an important step in everyone's career. Ask students to discuss the six items and number them in order of importance.

Answers

> There isn't one correct order, but *speak clearly* and *listen* are very important pieces of interview advice.

■ **Listening** *Presenting yourself at an interview*

1 Check if any students have attended a job interview. Ask if anyone has attended one in English! Tell students they are going to hear Michel Laval being interviewed for a chef's job. Ask them to read through questions 1–6. Check comprehension. Tell students to answer the questions as they listen, and play the recording. Let students compare their answers in pairs. Play the recording again, pausing if necessary for students to write down the answers. Go over the answers with the whole class.

Answers

> 1 Lyon　　　　　　　4 he wants to learn new menus
> 2 a chef's certificate　　and work with a new head chef
> 3 the Mercure Hotel　5 three
> 　　　　　　　　　　6 make a shortlist

2 Ask students to read sentences 1–7. Tell students to predict the missing words, and then check and correct their answers as they listen. Play the recording. Let students compare their answers in pairs. Go over the answers with the whole class.

Answers

> 1 lived　　3 hard-working　5 seeing　　　7 'll
> 2 like　　 4 experience　　 6 going to make

Ask students to turn to the Listening script on page 75 and read the interview. Model difficult and important phrases and structures, getting students to repeat chorally and individually. Students practise reading the interview in pairs, swapping roles. Go around and monitor their performance, helping where necessary. If students have difficulty with pronunciation and intonation, make a note of any problem areas and model these again afterwards, asking students to repeat after you. When students have practised enough, you could ask them to close their books and try to improvise the interview from memory.

■ **Language study**

Expressions to learn

Point out that I after each expression stands for *interviewer*. Ask students to read the expressions aloud, and check their pronunciation and intonation. Ask them to learn the expressions for homework.

New words to use

Ask students to read the words aloud and check pronunciation. Tell them to check any unfamiliar words in the Wordlist. Ask the class to learn the list of words for homework.

Structures to practise

Talking about the future

Explain there are a number of ways of talking about the future in English. Read through the examples with the students and explain the ways in which the forms are used:

- The Present Continuous is used to talk about arrangements, and is usually used with a future time phrase: *tomorrow, next week*, etc. It is often used with the verbs *go* and *come*: *I'm going to Paris tomorrow.* Give and elicit more examples: *What are you doing at the weekend? I'm going to my cousin's. / Are you coming to the cinema with us? What time are you leaving?*
- *going to* is used to talk about future intentions and decisions. The intention or decision expressed with *going to* is sometimes less certain or specific than the plan expressed with the Present Continuous. Give and elicit more examples: *We're going to move to New York. / I'm going to get a job in Valencia. / When are you going to finish the assignment?*
- *will* is used when you decide to do something at the time of speaking: *I'll phone you on Thursday. / We'll discuss the work rotas tomorrow. / We'll hire a car.* It is also used to forecast or predict future events; when you offer to do something; or when you promise to do something. Give and elicit more examples: *I think Brazil will win the next World Cup. / I'll take your coat for you. / I'll give him the message.*

3 Ask students to read questions 1–6. Check comprehension. Tell them to ask and answer questions in pairs. Check the use of the forms and give them vocabulary where necessary. Encourage students to improvise on the questions given.

■ **Listening** *A celebrity chef*

4 Tell students they are going to hear a celebrity chef, Jamie Oliver, being interviewed about his career so far. Ask them if they know anything about him. Tell students to read the ten sentences. Check comprehension and pronunciation. Ask students to work in pairs and try to predict the correct order of Jamie's responses before they listen. Play the recording. Let students check their answers in pairs. Play the recording again. Go over the answers with the whole class.

Answers

1 I was born in Essex …	6 After that, I worked at the River Café …
2 My dad runs a pub …	7 I've made three TV series …
3 When I was sixteen …	8 I've written four books …
4 After that, I went to France …	9 It'll be about my restaurant …
5 I was head pastry chef …	10 Definitely. I'm going to be the head chef.

5 Get students to work in pairs taking turns to interview each other. They should start by asking their partner questions about his or her past, then their present situation, and finally their hopes and plans for the future. Refer students back to the questions in exercise 3.

■ **Activity**

Tell students they are going to practise interviewing each other for hotel and restaurant jobs. If necessary, revise important words and information needed. Divide the class into pairs, Student A and Student B. Direct them to the correct page for each role, reminding them not to look at the other student's information. There is quite a lot of information, so students need to be given plenty of time to think about why they want this position, what qualities they will bring to it, as well as interview questions. Go around the class, helping students where necessary. When they have read the information and examples, ask Student B to begin by saying: *Tell me something about yourself.* Again, go around helping where necessary. Encourage them to note down the important information. Remind students the roles are then reversed and Student B is the applicant. When they have finished, students can discuss if they would have given each other the job or not, and why. Finally, go over general problems with the class, particularly any difficulties asking appropriate questions and giving full answers.

More words to use

Read the Family words and ask students to repeat after you. Tell them to check any unfamiliar words in the Wordlist. Read through the interview tips with the students and check comprehension. Ask them to study the list for discussion at the next lesson or a time when you are doing interview practice with them.

Unit 28 The interview

OXFORD
UNIVERSITY PRESS

Great Clarendon Street, Oxford OX2 6DP

Oxford University Press is a department of the University of Oxford.
It furthers the University's objective of excellence in research, scholarship,
and education by publishing worldwide in

Oxford New York

Auckland Cape Town Dar es Salaam Hong Kong Karachi
Kuala Lumpur Madrid Melbourne Mexico City Nairobi
New Delhi Shanghai Taipei Toronto

With offices in

Argentina Austria Brazil Chile Czech Republic France Greece
Guatemala Hungary Italy Japan Poland Portugal Singapore
South Korea Switzerland Thailand Turkey Ukraine Vietnam

OXFORD and OXFORD ENGLISH are registered trade marks of
Oxford University Press in the UK and in certain other countries

© Oxford University Press 2004

The moral rights of the author have been asserted

Database right Oxford University Press (maker)

First published 2004
2014 2013 2012 2011
10 9

No unauthorized photocopying

All rights reserved. No part of this publication may be reproduced,
stored in a retrieval system, or transmitted, in any form or by any means,
without the prior permission in writing of Oxford University Press,
or as expressly permitted by law, or under terms agreed with the appropriate
reprographics rights organization. Enquiries concerning reproduction
outside the scope of the above should be sent to the ELT Rights Department,
Oxford University Press, at the address above

You must not circulate this book in any other binding or cover
and you must impose this same condition on any acquirer

Any websites referred to in this publication are in the public domain and
their addresses are provided by Oxford University Press for information only.
Oxford University Press disclaims any responsibility for the content

ISBN-13: 978 0 19 457464 8

Typeset by Oxford University Press
in Minion

Printed in China